THE ENGINEERING OF
Breakfast Cereals and Inkjet Printers

An Unlikely Story of how I became
an Engineer at Kellogg's and HP

Tim Strecker, Ph.D.

WESTBOW
P R E S S®
A DIVISION OF THOMAS NELSON
& ZONDERVAN

WestBow Press books may be ordered through booksellers or by contacting:

WestBow Press
A Division of Thomas Nelson & Zondervan
1663 Liberty Drive
Bloomington, IN 47403
www.westbowpress.com
844-714-3454

ISBN: 978-1-6642-2373-8 (sc)
ISBN: 978-1-6642-2374-5 (e)

Library of Congress Control Number: 2021902957

Print information available on the last page.

WestBow Press rev. date: 05/10/2021

I would like to dedicate this to my parents, Will and Barbara Strecker, whose never ending love and support gave me the confidence to pursue a career in science and engineering

CONTENTS

INTRODUCTION

This is an unlikely story about how I became a research engineer at two iconic companies, Kellogg's and HP. Unlikely because there was nothing in my family, education, or intellect, that could have predicted I would ever get a graduate degree in chemical engineering and go on to have a successful, innovative career as an engineer at these companies. My childhood was in a lower, middle class family with no special privileges that come from wealth, connections, and business savvy. My family was supportive, nurturing, and loving, but I was never encouraged to pursue a college education or engineering as a career, though both my parents were college educated, because they were too poor to pay for my college education. Since my dad was a high school science teacher, there were no corporate and business influences during my formative years. There were no engineers in my immediate or extended family, so there were no role models or mentors for me to emulate and follow. My education was at a public high school, community college, and state university; no ivy league college education to give me an advantage over other potential engineering candidates at these companies. So, nothing could have predicted how my career and life turned out the way it did from looking at my upbringing, education, and life experiences.

I include my formative years, so you get a glimpse of how ordinary my life was in some respects and unique in others. Was there a clue that I might turn out to be an engineer? I also go into some depth about my college education since I was not a traditional college student. I did not start my education for a bachelor's degree until I was twenty-six years old and had a family. I would not finish graduate school until I was thirty-seven! I started my first job at Kellogg's right after completing graduate school at an age when most people are almost at their mid-career point, so my age was not a good indicator that I would amount to much at either of these companies.

So then, how did I become a successful and innovative research engineer at Kellogg's and HP? This is my story! Read on!

NO ONE IS BORN AN ENGINEER

"Go West, Young Man"

Life started for me on June 26, 1956 on the east coast in a small town of Asheville in western North Carolina located in the foothills of the Smokey Mountains. I was the first of five children that my parents, Will and Barbara Strecker, would have. Neither of my parents were from that part of the country. Dad grew up in Russell, Kansas, the middle son of three boys. Grandpa Strecker was a second generation of Germans in which his great grandparents had immigrated from Little Russia (now part of Ukraine) to Kansas. Grandpa Strecker's ancestors, though, had originally come from north central Germany and immigrated to Little Russia to avoid mandatory military service and taxes. He was a wheat farmer and they had a quarter section of land. Mom grew up in Kenmore, Washington, a suburb of the greater Seattle metropolitan area. She was the second oldest of four children and the only daughter. Grandpa Rediske was a businessman and jack of all trades who drove delivery trucks and did other odd jobs. Dad was a WWII vet who served in the U.S. Navy in the Pacific. After his enlistment, he used his GI bill to go to college where he majored in biology and got a teaching degree. Dad and mom met at college in South Carolina and then married after dad graduated. They moved to Savannah, Georgia where dad got his first teaching position. They then moved to Asheville a year later to a new teaching position at a private high school and I was born a year later. We moved to Wichita, Kansas after my younger brother was born. My sister was born in Wichita. We stayed in Kansas for a couple of years before moving out to Seattle, WA to be closer to my mom's parents, Grandpa and Grandma Rediske, and where dad got another teaching position at a high school in north Seattle. All the moving was done by car and a moving truck dad drove. After we arrived in Washington state, my two youngest brothers were born. I was four years old by the time we moved to Seattle. So, in the short time between when I was born and had arrived in Seattle, I had traversed the entire continent of the U.S., which, for that time when air travel was not very common, was a lot of moving!

Trees, Mountains, and Rain

I guess I was like anybody else growing up. Mostly a normal kid, doing normal things like going to school, throwing dirt clods at my friends in simulated battles in the backyard, riding bicycles, building tree houses, and getting in trouble.

Me in grade school.

Living in the Pacific Northwest in the Puget Sound area where Seattle, Tacoma, and Everett are located had its own unique challenges and qualities. One challenge was learning how to play outside when it rained six months out of the year. Mind you, the rain in Washington State is more of a constant drizzle than a heavy downpour one finds in other parts of the country, so we could usually play outside without getting drenched within minutes, but we did eventually get drenched after spending hours in the drizzle. A quality of the Puget Sound area is the abundance of trees. We climbed trees, made tree houses, road trees down to the ground after being cut down (OK, so I wasn't completely normal), had trails through tops of vine maple forests, and would hang on a branch to lower us to the ground from twenty feet up like an elevator. Trees were just a big part of life growing up, and a lot of my friends ended up working for lumber and paper mills in Everett after high school, so companies with tree-based products could also be a career. But I'm getting ahead of myself! Back to growing up and being mostly normal.

Family Matters

I lived in a family with five siblings and parents who were loving and nurturing.

My siblings and parents (I'm upper right).

My dad was a high school science teacher, and my mom was a homemaker who had a love of music. Their influence in creating an interest in both science and music was instrumental in my career as a future engineer. I remember many dinner conversations where Dad would tell us interesting tidbits about science and how things worked. He had a degree in biology and taught high school biology, physical science, and other miscellaneous courses since he taught at a small high school. So, during dinner he would tell us about everything from how the human body works to astronomy, geology, and meteorology. It created a natural curiosity in us about how things work and exploring the world we lived in. Dad was also quite the handyman and remodeled every house we lived in. He was good at repairing washing machines, dryers, lawn mowers, and cars. He taught me to not be afraid to try something new even if I didn't know anything about it, so that gave me the confidence to make things, tear things apart to see how they worked, and fix mechanical things. Mom was the musical one of the family. Dad couldn't carry a tune in a bucket. Mom had an angelic voice and loved to sing around the house, in church, and anywhere actually. She encouraged us to learn how to play a musical instrument. My mom's dad, Grandpa Rediske, played the saxophone in a military band and passed on the love of music to his daughter who, in turn, passed it on to us, her children. I don't remember how my interest in the violin started, but that is what I decided I wanted to learn to play when I was in second grade. Mom found a good violin music teacher, and that started my journey of private lessons for almost eight years. I developed a perfect pitch since you must play by ear on the violin. There are no frets, like on a guitar, to provide a place where your fingers are always in the correct tonal location, so placement on the violin had to be done by hearing the correct tone for that note. The trombone requires a similar approach since the slide is moved to achieve the correct tone and it is also requires having perfect pitch. In my violin-playing years Mom would take me occasionally to hear the Seattle Symphony Orchestra. That's like taking a kid to a candy shop for an aspiring violinist like myself. I read all the books about the classical music greats like Mozart, Beethoven, Strauss, Bach, Schubert, and Wagner in elementary school (that's normal, right?). I had a vision of becoming a world-class violinist someday, and I immersed myself in the lives of classical composers and musicians. As I got into middle school, playing the guitar became more of an interest because it was "cooler." And it was much easier to play than the violin because of the aforementioned frets.

My creative side.

I appreciated the musician's creativity, discipline, and accuracy in playing a musical instrument. To be good you need to have all three of those qualities. So, playing the violin and the guitar also prepared me for having these qualities as an engineer. I played music throughout my years in school—first through seventh grade were violin and eighth through twelfth were guitar and stereos. I played in a youth symphony one summer in middle school, and in high school I played electric guitar in a swing band. I continued to play guitar throughout my adult life informally with jam bands and such. I appreciated the creative effort needed to play an instrument, and I believe that helped me later as I went into engineering to think both creatively and analytically.

Inklings of Geekiness?

Another thing I did growing up that showed an inkling of my engineering future was how much I loved Lincoln Logs, Erector Sets, and as I got older in elementary school, making plastic model cars, planes, and ships. A friend of mine got me started putting plastic airplane models together since he had made dozens of WWII fighter and bomber models. So, my first WWII airplane model was a B17 Flying Fortress. If you've never built a plastic model of any kind before, it's a box full of molded plastic parts that you glue together following a set of instructions. It takes time, being meticulous, and sometimes you get high from the glue! The glue was nasty stuff. It smelled bad, got on my fingers, my clothes, on the plastic parts where I didn't want it, and on kitchen table, which did not make Mom very happy. Usually, all the plastic parts are one color, so you end up painting some parts of the model the color you want it to be to make it look more authentic. I went on to make many WWII planes, and I would then hang them from the ceiling in the bedroom, so it looked like a dog fight (that's what they call it when fighter planes were trying to blow each other out of the sky). I then moved onto model ships that were usually battleships and aircraft carriers. The last type of models I did were cars, usually hot rods like souped-up Ford Model Ts or Model As with large V8 engines, lots of chrome, and big loud exhaust pipes for show and sound. As I got closer to middle school, the hormones began to kick in, and the model building days were numbered. All the models I built ended their existence in one of three ways: being blown up with firecrackers, shot to pieces with a BB gun, or set on fire with model glue as the primer! Looking back, I wished I would have kept them, but as a kid what fun would that have been when they could be destroyed in such creative and dramatic ways!

Model train sets and car racing sets were a big part of our lives growing up too. We had a Lionel train set as very young kids before starting school and loved the smell of the ozone the electric motors gave off when running them. As we got older, we liked the faster electric racecar sets that were available then. We would sit for hours racing the cars around tracks set up in the family room. The racetracks would allow two racecars to run side by side, so we would see how fast we could go until they would fly off the track going around a corner or run into each other and knock one of the cars out of the race. It provided hours of entertainment, and inadvertently, we also learned how to design track layouts and set up the cars with softer rubber tires to grip the track better so they could go faster without slipping.

I grew up spending a lot of time building things or playing with toys that required something more than just entertainment—like design, mechanical aptitude, and being creative.

Just an Average Student

I was an average student throughout elementary, middle, and high school. I was more interested in music, girls, and cars than schoolwork. I was not prime engineering material in anyone's wildest imaginations, especially my teachers'. There were periods in school where I did excel, especially in science fair projects in elementary school. One project I did was make a working model of a building elevator that went up and down between multiple floors. It was manually operated using pulleys and strings, but it was fun figuring out how to make it work. In high school I got interested in metal shop and electronics. My interest in electronics came out of my love of stereos. My younger brother and I shared a bedroom growing up, and in high school we got interested in stereos, since we liked listening to music loudly. So naturally that led us to finding the biggest and loudest stereos we could afford at the time. My first stereo was a Sansui 8080 receiver and amp (which I still have by the way) that could deliver 80 watts per channel to a pair of Bose 501 speakers. All of this was in a bedroom about twelve-by-twelve feet in size. We could get the walls vibrating with that stereo. Our favorite pastime was visiting local stereo stores in Seattle and Everett and drooling over the high-end stereo equipment we saw in them. One store had a basement room with no windows for their high-end stereos because these bad boys were so powerful it would blow out the storeroom windows on the main floor! Our jean pant legs would flutter when this stereo was turned up. I don't remember the amp they were using but it was using Klipsch speakers that were almost as tall as we were. It was also in high school that I became interested in cars and learned how to work on cars since my first car needed a lot of work to keep it running. It was a '57 Chevy Belaire two door hardtop.

My first car

The body was in perfect shape, but the automatic transmission had been replaced with a three-speed manual transmission and it was always breaking down. So, I learned how to take the transmission out and take it to a mechanic who could replace the bearings that seemed to wear out too soon. One day I was trying to show off to my neighbor buddies by revving up the engine, popping the clutch, and "burning rubber". If you've ever been to a fuel dragster or funny car event you know exactly what "burning rubber" means. They get the back tires spinning and literally burn the rubber off the tires to warm them up so they will get more traction off the starting line. So, here I was, trying to do this with my '57 Chev to show how much power it had. It really was a gutless car. It had a small block 283 cubic inch stock V8 that had no modifications to increase its horsepower or performance. So, when I popped the clutch and revved it up all I heard was a loud clank and the car sat still! I got out and looked under the car to see one end of the drive shaft hanging down. All I had done was broke the u-joint that connects the drive shaft to the back of the transmission, so the car couldn't be driven at all. So, my friends helped me push it back to my house where I then got to work replacing the u-joint. That was embarrassing! But I did get good at fixing cars and learning about hands on mechanics along the way and not being afraid to tear into something without knowing anything about it beforehand. My next two cars, which I wish I still had now too along with the '57 Chev, were a '67 Chevelle, and a '69 Dodge Charger. All these cars are now classics and worth a lot more money than when I had them, but I wasn't going to be a car collector, I was going to be an engineer! To become an engineer, it would be a journey through working as a technician, years of college, graduate school, and eventually my first engineering job.

ELECTRONICS AND BICYCLES

Guitar Amps and Stereos

I first developed an interest in electronics when in high school through my love of music and stereos. I built a guitar amp from a design I found, bought the parts, and put it together. It ended up being a "whimpy" amp in that it wasn't all that powerful, and I wasn't able to blast the windows out of my bedroom window playing my electric guitar, but it did get me interested in electronics in the process. I decided in high school that it would be fun and interesting to become an electronic technician and work on electronic gadgets like a guitar amplifier or electronic instruments as a profession, so I decide to get an electronic technician degree after I graduated from high school. I initially went to a private vocational school like the ones they have today such as ITT Technical Institute for a year before transferring to Mount Vernon Community

College to get an associate degree in electronic technician. It was at Mount Vernon Community College that I had my first exposure to a computer in 1975, in this case, a mainframe computer and it was in 1977 that personal computers started becoming available and popular such as the Apple II and Tandy Radio Shack TRS-80. We had to use punch cards to program the mainframe computer. The instructor would put intentional faults in the punch cards, and we would have to troubleshoot the code or cards in this case to see where the error was. It was a great experience of learning how to troubleshoot a problem on something new without any prior experience.

My First High Tech Job

I completed my associate degree at Mount Vernon in 1975 and got a job immediately with an aerospace electronics company, Eldec, in north Seattle area near Lynnwood. I supported the production line for military electronic components to make proximity sensors and, later, power supplies for the heads up displays in F14 fighter jets. I worked a lot with the design engineers in troubleshooting problems on the production line where I would conduct final testing on the products. My first job at Eldec was testing and troubleshooting proximity sensors used on jets to indicate landing gear and wing flap positions for the pilots. These sensors would provide pilots with confirmation that the landing gear had retracted all the way into the fuselage after takeoff and then on landing would provide confirmation that the landing gear were in the fully extended position and locked for landing. The wing flap sensors would give pilots the position of the flaps so that they were sure they were where they thought they were supposed to be. We did a lot of reliability testing of these sensors to make sure they would not fail prematurely on the aircraft. One of my first responsibilities was to test the sensors in extreme cold and heat environments using special chambers which could ramp down to -100 F and up to 300 F. Liquid carbon dioxide was used to cool the chambers down. Once the liquid carbon dioxide was injected into the chambers it would turn to gas immediately and cool the temperature down in minutes. The chambers were not airtight so some of the carbon dioxide would leak out. There were many chambers the size of large microwave ovens lined up on both sides of an aisle in the test area. I would monitor progress and remove and add more components into test as needed. When I first started working in this test area, I couldn't figure out why I was so tired all the time. One of my coworkers said it was because the carbon dioxide concentration in that aisle was higher, so my oxygen level was lower, making me feel tired. Well, after a year of doing that I moved to a different job in another product area working on heads up display power supplies and, bingo, I wasn't tired anymore! My new job was working on final testing of the heads-up display power supplies used on F14 fighter jets. On one occasion, I was troubleshooting a power supply that wasn't working correctly and I had the design engineer who had designed it working with me to figure out what the problem was. We were checking the printed circuit board for voltage levels to see where it was failing and suddenly, we heard a loud "Pop!" and confetti blowing up in our faces! What had happened was a line assembler had placed an electrolytic capacitor in backwards. Electrolytic capacitors have a specific polarity and if put into the board backwards, it will not allow the current to flow and will overheat and eventually blow up like a firecracker, which is exactly what this one did. The engineer and I immediately jumped backwards when it blew up. We were not hurt, just startled, and we immediately started laughing about it. It was an easy fix to replace the capacitor and have it pass assembly testing. Not all problems were this obvious and easy to fix. Some were tough to figure out and not as obvious as the capacitor problem. I would eventually use my troubleshooting skills I learned as a technician in my engineering career.

Seeing Europe on a Bicycle

You might wonder how this is relevant to my story of becoming an engineer. It's part of who I am and why I almost went into full time ministry instead of engineering. I was living with a high school friend, Dan Eylander, in Lake Stevens when I was working at Eldec. He had bought his parent's house when he graduated from high school and was looking for a roommate. I jumped at the chance to finally be able to live on my own and moved in shortly after starting work at Eldec. We eventually had five roommates as the house had enough room for all of us. One day the five of us were sitting around on a weekend talking about fun things we could do and the idea of seeing Europe by bicycle came up. We got the idea from meeting a young man who had bicycled through North and South America and thought that would be a fun way to see Europe. So, we set a goal of going to Europe in a year from then. At the time three of us had steady jobs and the other two were employed part time with sporadic jobs, but we all decided to try to go together within a year. Well, as time went on it became apparent that the guys with the sporadic jobs were not going to make it, and one of the guys with a steady job decided to stay home. So, it was Dan and I who eventually ended up going to Europe for six months touring on bicycles and trains. Dan had met a Norwegian girl in the states who invited us to stay with her and her parents before we started our bicycle tour the summer in 1977. They lived on a small island, Askoy, off the coast of Norway across the bay from Bergen. It was a similar distance from Everett to Whidbey Island or from Seattle to Bainbridge Island if you're familiar with the Puget Sound area of Washington State. We stayed with the family on Askoy for two months and it was a great way to get in shape for our upcoming bike trip. Askoy and Bergen are at the same latitude as Anchorage, Alaska, so during the summer we were there, we experienced our first time with midnight sun. The rooms had darkening shades so we could sleep through the bright nights. One of our favorite times with our host family was the after-dinner dessert times when they would invite neighbors and friends over to meet the two Americans staying at their place for the summer. They would have a spread of desserts on the coffee table in the living room and every one of them was delicious. For a couple of young men with appetites all the time, this was like heaven on earth! We were able to easily burn off the calories since we spent hours cycling around Askoy Island to get in shape for our bike trip later in the summer. We started our bike trip in August. Since we were in Norway, we didn't want to leave too close to the cooler weather of fall and needed to get south far enough to stay out of the winter weather. Our first goal was to ride from Bergen to Oslo in eastern Norway, just short of three hundred miles but over a major mountain range in western Norway, not far from Bergen. We would try to ride around fifty miles per day and had a two-man backpack tent that we camped in wherever we could find a spot to set it up. From Oslo we traveled to Jonkoping, Sweden, at the southern end of Lake Vattern. Dan had some contacts there that we ended up staying with for about a week before heading down to Denmark where we stayed in Copenhagen. From Copenhagen we traveled to Kiel, Germany and then rode across northern Germany into the Netherlands. We rode through the Netherlands, Belgium, and then into Luxembourg. It took about two months to travel over 1,500 miles from Bergen, Norway to Luxembourg. By the time we arrived in Luxembourg, fall had set in with its cooler temperatures and frequent wet weather like what we were used to in the Pacific Northwest this time of year. So, we decided to head back to Bergen to see our host family again and decide how we wanted to see the rest of Europe. We traveled back to Bergen by train with our bikes in the luggage car. Once we get back to Askoy, we started planning the next phase of our trip to see the rest of Europe. We were leaning on getting Interrail train passes available in Europe at the time, similar to Euro passes we could have purchased in the U.S. So, that is what we ended up doing and spent another two months traveling central and southern Europe by train. We ended up traveling to most of the western European countries including England and Scotland and one eastern European country, then called Yugoslavia (now made up of six separate republics: Slovenia, Bosnia, Croatia, Montenegro, Serbia, and North Macedonia). The only southern European countries we didn't visit were Portugal and Greece. It was during this part of our trip that we spent a week at a castle in Bavaria, Germany. It was a training center for short term missionaries, and we were interested in doing something like that in the future. So, we spent the week there mingling with the students and sitting in on lectures. I would eventually join this ministry back in the states a few years later and spend three years with them. Dan and I spent six months in Europe. It was the trip of a lifetime and I am so grateful that I was able to do this while I was young and single. Speaking of being single, I did have a girlfriend during this time, Connie Morin, who I met about six months before going to Europe. She was excited about the trip for me, but we did miss each other a lot. We kept up a steady stream of letters back and forth while I was in Europe. I had quite a stack of letters that I brought back home which Connie had written while I was in Europe.

Maiwage and Twue Wove (a quote from the movie Princess Bride)

I went back to work for Eldec again once I got back home. Connie still worked there as an assembler before I went on my trip and while I was gone. We picked up where we had left off when I went to Europe and we started to talk about getting married. A little over two years later we were married on February 3, 1979.

I married up!

In the winter of 1978, I went to work for Fluke Instruments in Everett, WA where I worked as an end of the line final assembly test technician and worked there until the spring of 1979 after we were married. I then went to work for the calibration labs at General Telephone in Mukilteo, called GTE at that time, where I worked on testing and calibration of the instruments GTE used to keep the phone switching equipment working at the central office or telephone switching station. I worked at GTE for a little over a year. In the spring of 1980, Connie and I moved to Tacoma, WA to work for a Christian mission's organization and were considering going into full time ministry. It was the same mission's organization which had the training center in the castle in Bavaria that I had visited three years earlier. We helped with resettling Southeast Asian refugees from Cambodia and Laos. During this time in Tacoma, both of our children, Leah and Luke, were born. It was also during this time that I started to think about going back to college and pursuing an engineering degree. I felt that full time work was more of my calling than full time ministry, though it was initially a struggle to come to that realization[1]. I was initially interested in electrical engineering since I had been an electronic technician. I investigated the curriculum and talked to an advisor at Tacoma Community College (TCC) which had a great engineering transfer program with both University of Washington (UW) and Washington State University (WSU). The advisor reviewed my transcripts and said the only class that would transfer to an electrical engineering degree was my English comp class! So, I had to basically start from the beginning since I had never taken chemistry, physics, or math beyond geometry in high school. So, I signed up for classes at TCC in the fall of 1982 and didn't realize at the time that I would be in college for the next twelve years!

A NON-TRADITIONAL COLLEGE STUDENT

Undergraduate Life

College life as a twenty-six-year-old husband and father of two young children was not the typical student in college in the early 1980s. I started taking classes full time at Tacoma Community College (TCC) in the fall of 1982. Our daughter, Leah, had been born about a year earlier and our son would come along in another year during my second year at TCC. It was challenging and mentally invigorating to go back to college eight years after graduating from high school. Since I had to take a lot of prerequisite classes to even start the regular engineering curriculum I felt behind and overwhelmed, but I just put one foot in front of the other and started out on this wild and whacky adventure! The prerequisites I had to take were primarily math and science classes as I mentioned earlier: college algebra, trigonometry, inorganic chemistry, introductory organic chemistry, and introductory physics. Once I got these out of the way then I could start taking the regular engineering classes such as calculus, organic chemistry, physics, and pre-engineering classes such as statics and dynamics, strength of materials, and computer programming classes such as Fortran. I gained more confidence as I took each class realizing that I could grasp the concepts and excel in them. I had to study harder than recent high school graduates who I usually took classes with, but I was able to not only pass them but usually got A's or B's in them. I spent three years at TCC where most students who had all the prerequisites done in high school could complete it in two years. I received an Associate's Degree in Science from TCC and began to make preparations for going to Washington State University in Pullman, Washington.

One funny story I must tell you occurred after I had sent my admission application to WSU as part of the transfer process from TCC to WSU. I started to receive invitations to come to Pullman and visit various fraternities! Apparently, they either didn't read my application information very carefully or weren't able to get my personal information in the application and, thus, didn't know that I was married with two young children. My wife and I had a good laugh about those invitations and remarked that we should show up with the "fam" and see their reaction! But we decided not to follow through …

We moved from Tacoma to Pullman in the summer of 1985. We had both grown up in western Washington state, which was the milder, greener, wetter side of the state in the larger metropolitan areas of Seattle, Tacoma, and Everett located next to Puget Sound. The state is divided in two by the Cascade mountain range with western Washington and eastern Washington which is the dryer, more extreme temperatures in the summer and winter, and not as many trees and lush greenery. Eastern Washington is also more rural and agricultural with much less population than the western part of the state. Tacoma had a population of several hundred thousand and Pullman was around twenty thousand including the students. So, it was quite an adjustment for us to move to Pullman. The largest city in eastern Washington is Spokane about seventy-five miles north of Pullman and was about the size of Tacoma. We drove to Spokane as often as we could so that we could get back to a large city setting which we missed being in the small little farming town of Pullman, which happened to have the second largest university, WSU, in Washington located there. By the time we left Pullman almost ten years later, we had gotten used to the small-town feel and eastern Washington climate and geography, but the first few years in Pullman were a struggle for us.

I had to declare an engineering major when I applied to WSU. As I said earlier, I had originally wanted to pursue an electrical engineering degree but by the time

I had completed my studies at TCC I had changed it to Agricultural Engineering. Wow! You might think that is quite a change of direction since these two engineering degrees are about as far apart as they could be with electrical engineering being very high tech and agricultural engineering being very low tech and back to the earth. Well, you're right! What made me change my mind was a professor from Purdue University who was a guest lecturer at the nonprofit group I was working with for refugee resettlement efforts. They also had an appropriate technology division that focused on designing technologies for developing countries that met needs they had which didn't need high tech, complex solutions, but ones that were "appropriate" for their needs and requirements. One product they developed was a grain thresher powered by humans riding a bicycle. They developed many other products and technologies that met the needs of these developing countries that the local people could easily use and make them more productive. The Purdue professor lectured at the appropriate technology division and trained them in agriculture and technologies that were needed. I heard what he was teaching on and became interested in it, so I made an appointment to go see him and ask him about which engineering degree he would recommend for this area. He recommended agricultural engineering. I investigated the degree program at WSU, and it had two major options. One was in food process engineering where the focus was on the process equipment design required for food production such as cereal, or baked goods, etc. The other option was in irrigation and water engineering. I decided that food process engineering would be the path I would focus on. So, that's how I arrived at my decision to pursue agricultural engineering instead of electrical engineering. Another aspect of my decision to pursue agricultural engineering was based on my experience with the Southeast Asian refugees I had come to know and be friends with during my time of helping many resettle in the Tacoma area. They had come from an agrarian society and I wanted to help people in developing countries become more self-sufficient and use appropriate technologies to make their agriculture more productive and nutritious. So, when I applied to go to WSU, I declared my major as agricultural engineering. I would change my major one more time when I went to graduate school, but I'm getting ahead of myself. I will go into more details on that later.

I continued to study hard and excel in my college courses once I arrived at WSU, but my first semester wasn't a good indicator initially that I would even make it one semester. I took a full load the first semester. One course I had to take as an agricultural engineer was a fluid mechanics class in the mechanical engineering department. It was considered a weed-out class in the mechanical engineering department, meaning, it was very difficult, and many would not only drop out of the course but out of mechanical engineering all together when they couldn't pass it! There were only two exams during the semester: a mid-term and final exam. The mid-term had six story problems to solve. I looked at the first problem and didn't have a clue on how to solve it. I looked at the second problem and didn't have a clue on how to solve it. I started to panic. I looked at the next four problems and didn't have a clue how to solve any of them. Now I was really sweating! So, I went back to the first problem and started to list all the assumptions I thought would be needed to solve it. I stated how I thought it might be solved with these assumptions. I then did the same thing for all the other five problems. Mind you, I didn't solve a single problem for the exam, I didn't come up with a solution or an answer for any of them. One of the good things about engineering exams and homework is that how you solve it is just as important as getting the right answer. Showing your assumptions and how you set up the problem is just as important as getting the correct number. It shows you understand the concepts even if you don't get a right number. So, for the fluid mechanics mid-term, I got forty-one points out of hundred by just stating my assumptions and how I might set up the problem to solve it. The average for that exam was twenty-nine! So, I did okay, but it was still a huge let down to only score forty-one points on my first engineering exam at WSU. It didn't instill much confidence that I was going to make it in engineering by any stretch of the imagination. The good news is that I did much better on the final exam and ended up with a B+ in the class! You also need to understand that agricultural engineering students were usually viewed as the flunkies by the other engineering programs such as electrical, mechanical, and chemical engineering students since the perception was that only farming kids went into agricultural engineering and they weren't as smart. So, I felt fairly good in beating out a lot of mechanical engineering students in the fluid mechanics class and passing it with a B+ while a lot of them flunked out or quit!

Food Engineering, Pasta Races, and Aseptic Processing

Food process engineers focuses on the engineering of processes, process equipment, and the entire process line required for food production. One process used in cereal production is an extruder, which I will go into more detail later since it was the focus of my Ph.D. research. Think of all the processed foods you eat. How did they get their shape, color, taste, and packaging to preserve and ship them in to get them to your table? During the low-fat craze of the mid 1990s a lot of engineering and science was used to produce low fat foods such as cream cheese, snacks such as chips and cookies, and desserts. How was this done? Food scientists and chemists figured out how to replace fat with things such as gums (xanthan, guar, lecithin, carrageenan, to name a few) to achieve the mouth feel, or texture that fats give food. They also had to add flavor enhancers to replace the flavors lost by removing the fats. There are flavor companies who do nothing but develop flavors from savory to sweet which are used in foods to add and enhance their flavors. Food chemists with expertise in flavor chemistry can make well over six figures a year in this industry. Once a low-fat food is developed, it then needs to be processed many times in a heating or cooling process, drying, forming, and packaging. This is where the food process engineer comes in and works with the food scientists and chemists to develop a proto process usually in a pilot plant or bench top process in a lab. Once the proto process has been developed, tested, and verified, then the engineer moves on to develop a scaled up full production process which will be used to produce the food product including packaging. This development can take months and years depending on the complexity and process equipment required. This example of low-fat food technology is just one of thousands that have been developed in the food industry where food process engineers have been involved in some pretty innovative and interesting development projects.

When I started my studies in the food process engineering department, they had an introductory party for the new students in the department early in the fall term before the weather turned cold. It was a pasta race! We met outside in the parking lot behind the engineering building where a number of folding tables were set up with boxes of different shaped pasta. The students were then formed into four to five different teams with each team getting a box of pasta shapes. The goal of the event was to make a pasta vehicle which would then be run down a ramp and the fastest vehicle would win the competition. Think of the box car roller derby that used to be part of Boy Scouts. This was similar but using pasta instead of wood. It involved creativity, teamwork, engineering judgement, innovation, and a lot of fun! I don't remember which team one and the design used, but I do remember that this was my first experience of using pasta to build a race car!

As I alluded above in the low-fat food example, there are many process steps used in food production:

- Heating
- Cooling
- Drying
- Food Additives
- Fermenting
- Packaging

There have also been many new process techniques developed over the last few decades that have advanced food processing:

Advances in Food Process Technology

Process Technology	Process Description	Benefits	Typical uses
Aseptic	Liquid product sterilized within two seconds then put into sterilized packaging	Preserves flavor, kills bacteria and pathogens, shelf-stable	Juices, milk
Freeze drying	Freeze, lower pressure, remove ice through sublimation	Food texture and flavor are preserved after rehydrating	Fruits, vegetables, dehydrated meals for outdoor and military use
Infrared heating	Uses infrared radiation to heat food	Faster heating resulting in less vitamin and flavor losses	Cereal baking, coffee roasting
Irradiation	Ionizing radiation kills bacteria, does not create radioactive food	Prevents foodborne illnesses, reduces food spoilage, increases shelf-life of fruits and vegetables	Meat, shell fish, fresh fruits and vegetables
Magnetic field	Subject food in sealed plastic bags to magnetic pulses	Used in food preservation by changing physiochemical, enzymatic, and microbiological characteristics	Aid in freezing blueberries to preserve their flavor and bioactive compounds

Microwave heating	Industrial microwave operate at 915 MHz and 2.45 GHz	Faster heating times	Cooking, drying, pasteurization, preservation
Modified atmosphere storage	Storage where the gas levels are modified from outside levels	Prevents fruits and meat from spoiling while in long-term storage	Meats and fruit
Ohmic heating	An electric current is passed through the food itself causing it to heat up	Heats a product rapidly and uniformly	Pasteurizing and sterilizing liquid and particulate foods
Pulsed electric field	High intensity pulsed electric field (20-80 kV/cm) to liquid foods passing between two electrodes	Rapid pasteurization of liquid foods	Juices, milk, liquid whole eggs
Spray drying	Method of producing a dry powder from a liquid or slurry	Simultaneous dehydration and micronized particle formation in one process	Milk powder, juice powder, flavor powders
Ultrasound	Sound waves create a mechanical vibration and cavitation which can be used for emulsification	Faster emulsion processing and stability	Ketchup, mayonnaise, sauces

I want to highlight one new technology above and that is aseptic processing. This is used for liquid food products such as milk and fruit juices which are shelf stable and don't require any refrigeration. It does not require in-container sterilization of liquid foods which usually takes a longer time (typically tens of minutes) than an aseptic process. Aseptic processing involves three primary steps: thermal sterilization of the liquid food (typically a couple of seconds), sterilization of the packaging material, and conserving this sterile environment during packaging. Since the liquid food has only experienced a very short time, high temperature process, flavor is preserved, and a shelf-stable product has been achieved. There have also been a lot of new technologies to address food safety during processing. Cold plasma is a recent innovation used to inactivate foodborne pathogens. Plasma is created by ionizing a feed gas such as argon, helium, or oxygen. This is done at room temperature, thus the "cold" plasma name. The cold plasma is very effective in sanitizing food and contact surfaces without heating or damaging the treated product. So, this gives you a little glimpse into the innovation, engineering, and science that goes into the foods we eat and enjoy.

Bachelor's Degree and Huckleberry Cordials

Since my major in agricultural engineering was food process engineering, the senior design project was to be focused on some aspect of engineering as it related to food production, whether it be food processing of processed food such as sauces, ready to eat food, snacks, baked goods, and candy; or food harvesting such as grains, vegetables, and fruit. All engineering disciplines included a senior design project during the last year of their bachelor's degree and I got to work on improving the process of huckleberry cordial candy making. Our department had been contacted by a company in Libby, Montana which made huckleberry cordials using wild huckleberries from the mountains around Libby. We traveled to Libby to visit them and they showed us their current cordial production process. We also got to sample the huckleberry cordials, which further motivated us to work on the project! They wanted to automate more of their candy making process since a lot of it was done by hand at the time. The most labor-intensive part of the process was forming the chocolate cordial shell that a huckleberry and syrup went into. A plastic molded sheet was used which had a dozen or so cavities where the cordial shape was formed into a half circle shaped shell. A small amount molten chocolate was poured into each cavity and then a small brush was used to coat each cavity with a thin layer of chocolate by hand. After that, a single huckleberry was placed into the chocolate shell with a small amount of syrup and a final coat of chocolate was added to seal the bottom of the cordial. Our project was to determine what process could be used to automate the coating of the cordial shaped mold sheet so that it would speed up the slow method of doing it manually by hand. The company sent us mold sheets and boxes of large chocolate baking chips used to make the cordial shells. When we saw the boxes of chocolate chips which were sent, we knew this was going to be a fun project since there was a lot of chocolate involved! We spent weeks making molten chocolate and replicating the existing hand coating process, so we understood the mechanics of the process. We also ate a lot of chocolate! Who said engineering was boring?! We spent a lot of time researching methods already used in industry for making coated candy and eventually came up with a spray nozzle process which would spray a coating of molten chocolate into each mold cavity. We used nozzles already available on the market and designed an array of nozzles so that a single sheet or multiple sheets could be coated in one process step, greatly increasing the process throughput and speed. And did I say, we ate a lot of chocolate in the process?! At the end of the project, the company attended our presentation at WSU and we showed them the equipment used in one of our labs. They liked the new, more automated process and planned to implement it as soon as they could. It was a great project because we learned about working as a team, brainstorming process design ideas, figuring out what the critical engineering parameters were important for spraying molten chocolate, putting together a presentation for communicating our results, and, ultimately, seeing it implemented in an actual food production process. These were all aspects of what we would experience as engineers in industry, so it was valuable preparation for engineers in training.

Cranberry Harvesting

During the summer between my bachelor's and master's degrees I was in Pullman and one of the professors had a project I was asked if I would be interested in. It was a mechanical cranberry harvester used to harvest cranberries from a cranberry bog. It had been designed by someone else in the department but never tested in the field, so they wanted someone to take it over to the cranberry bogs along the Washington State coast and conduct some tests to see how well it performed and to make recommendations on how to improve it if required. The cranberry harvester was a small machine about the size of a large walk behind rototiller where the harvester operator would walk behind it using two handles to control speed and direction.

Cranberry harvester picking mechanism

There were cutters on the front of the machine to prune and trim the cranberry plants while harvesting. The harvester had fingers or tines on the front end also near the cutters and these were used to gentle remove the ripe cranberries from the vine. Once the cranberries were removed by the tines, they immediately emptied into a conveyor which then dumped them into a burlap sack for storage until further cleaning and packaging could be done. It was a fairly simple harvester and the tests showed that it was doing a good job at both pruning and removing cranberries. Cranberries are harvested by two methods: dry harvesting using a machine similar to the one I was testing, and wet harvesting where the cranberry bog is flooded and the ripe cranberries float to the surface where they are then corralled and transported to containers using mobile conveying equipment. The testing showed that the harvester was working as expected and the cranberry farmers that I was running the tests with were happy with the results. Further testing was going to be done by a farmer over the harvest season to see how reliable the machine was. So, at that point, the summer project was completed.

Master's Degree and Apple Chemistry

I finished my undergraduate work in two years at WSU and decided to stay another year to get a master's degree in the same department. The master's degree topic was on how to determine the maturity level of apples using quantitative analysis such as a chemical marker that could be determined non-destructively. It had great implications for the apple industry because it would enable apple producers to sort apples by how ripe they were so that when they went into long-term storage they wouldn't spoil as quickly. It's really true that one "bad" apple can spoil the bunch! As apples grow, they produce and utilize ethylene gas, a natural plant hormone, to ripen and it increases the riper they are, so if you store a riper apple with a bunch of less ripe ones, the riper apple will trigger the other ones to start ripening as well. In other words, ethylene gas from the riper apples nearby causes the unripe apples to start ripening through a chain reaction so that an entire controlled atmospheric storage building of apples could spoil with massive economic losses to farmers. So, if a method could be developed to sort apples based on their ethylene gas levels or another chemical marker that was part of the ripening cycle of an apple, then that would be a huge benefit to the industry and reduce the amount of waste from over ripe apples. It was a lofty goal to find an easy and reliable method. I found a chemical marker called NADH, or Nicotinamide Adenine Dinucleotide, which was part of the biochemical cycle for apple ripening and it was fluorescent when illuminated with UV light. The only problem was that we needed a non-destructive method for sorting. When I illuminated the apple skin to the UV light there was abundant fluorescence from the apple skin due to other compounds that fluoresced as well, swamping out the NADH fluorescent signal. So, though NADH was a viable marker, it wouldn't work for this method of non-destructive detection, and that was the conclusion from the research for my master's degree. As a side note, ethylene gas couldn't be used for rapid sorting since an apple's gas emission is so small that it would have to be placed in a sealed chamber for some amount of time to allow the gas level to increase to a level detectable by a gas sniffer. With thousands of apples being sorted per hour and the need to determine each individual apple's maturity level, the gas detection method was much too slow.

Consulting at Nalley's Food

After completing my master's degree, I went to work as a consultant to a food company in Tacoma, Nalley's Food who made everything from pickles, soups, and chips. It was my first experience of working in the food processing industry, so it was a great first exposure to what types of work an engineer did in that industry. I was primarily doing a lot of industrial engineering work for things like time-and-motion studies to see where improvements could be made in the conveyor systems between process steps.

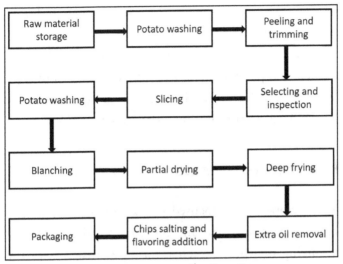

Potato chip production line flow diagram

I had to interact a lot with line operators and their supervisors, and it required using my people skills to gain their trust and confidence so they would let me out on their manufacturing lines to get my work done. At one point, one of the plant managers was upset that I didn't clear my work with him first. The director of engineering who I worked for didn't think it was necessary to get the plant manager's clearance first, but I learned a lot about the politics of operations like that and made sure I had the plant managers approval before any future work was done. I worked there for six months and then decided to return to WSU in Pullman to pursue a doctorate in engineering. Before going back to Pullman, I was looking for an engineering job in industry, but didn't find anything. I contacted my former advisor, Dr. Cavalieri, in the agricultural engineering department and told him of my interest in pursuing a doctorate degree and he immediately offered one to me which would be fully funded and pay for the degree and a stipend to live on. What a deal! I accepted it on the spot! So, me and the family headed off to Pullman once again.

Ph.D. and Cereal Chemistry

My doctorate work focused on extrusion processing of cereal grains and determining the chemical reactions occurring in wheat proteins during extrusion with the goal on eventually controlling the extrusion process more deterministically. Wheat flour consists of 70-75% starch, 10-14% protein depending on what variety it is, and the remaining being lipids and polysaccharides. Wheat proteins consist of gluten proteins and non-gluten proteins. Gluten proteins consist of two types: glutenin proteins which are the higher molecular weight fraction and gliadin proteins which are the lower molecular fraction. Gluten proteins are responsible for much of the texture formation during extrusion due to crosslinking. The non-gluten proteins consist of albumins, globulins, and amino acids.

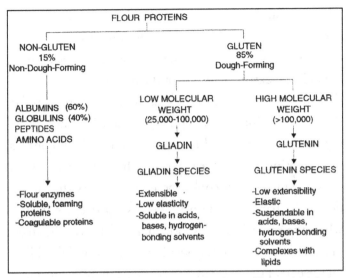

Various types of protein found in wheat flour. Gluten protein is responsible for most of the texture formation during extrusion

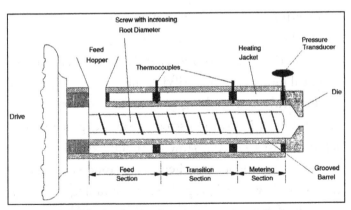

Industrial cereal extruder where raw ingredients are loaded into the hopper on the left-hand side of the picture, a rotating auger or screw inside mixes and cooks the mixture in a heated barrel, and the cooked cereal is forced out the die plate through shaped holes on the right-hand side of the picture to finish the process

That is, could processed cereal grain quality, extent of cooking, etc. be calculated by the process parameters set on the extruder such as temperate, screw speed, etc., etc.? Cereal extrusion is one of the methods of producing shaped breakfast cereal and has become more popular since it combines several processes into one step. Raw ingredients are inserted into the extruder which consists of a rotating auger screw inside a heated barrel which conveys, mixes, and cooks the ingredients as they move down the barrel. A die plate with shaped holes in it is where the cooked cereal is formed into shapes as the auger pushes it out through the openings. A rotating knife blade on the exit of the die plate then cuts the shaped cereal into individual pieces.

A material science approach to food science and engineering was emerging more and more during my Ph.D. research years. It leveraged the research that material scientists and chemists had used for the chemical industry in quantifying the material properties of chemicals and making process development more deterministic. Now, food scientists and engineers were beginning to apply the same methodologies developed by material scientists and chemists for food systems and processes. I was utilizing these methodologies in my research of food extrusion to understand the material properties and chemical reactions occurring in wheat protein and starch during extrusion. One aspect of food extrusion of cereals that was not well understood was the heat transfer coefficients and mechanisms controlling heat transfer during extrusion. Some of my research was to develop a method to determine these heat transfer properties of wheat protein and starch and use it to model what happens during extrusion[2,3]. Another area that was not well understood at all were the chemical reactions occurring in wheat protein and starch during extrusion.

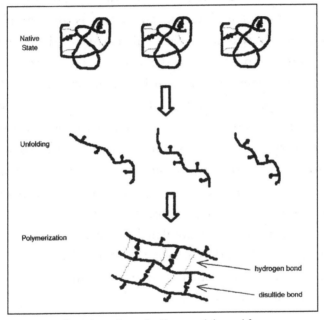

Protein polymerization model used for cereal extrusion modeling

It was known that the proteins and starches (complex carbohydrates) reacted with each other and created a crosslinked network similar to thermosetting polymers such as epoxies, but the reaction mechanisms and kinetics (the rate of reaction) were not well known or understood especially during the complex extrusion process where heat and shear were used to change the material properties of the wheat protein and starch. One innovation that I was able to develop during my research was an extrusion rheometer[4]. A rheometer is used to determine the rheology, or deformation and flow of non-Newtonian fluids. Water is an example of a Newtonian fluid. Peanut butter is an example of a non-Newtonian fluid. This extrusion rheometer enabled us to determine the viscosity (i.e., rheology) of wheat protein in an extrusion environment of both high temperature and high shear rates. We knew that the high temperature in an extruder would cause polymerization of the protein through disulfide bond formation, but there was a competing reaction occurring from the shear rate tearing these bonds apart. This extrusion rheometer provided a method to conduct a controlled test which simulated the melt section of an extruder without the complexities of the extruder screw geometry and unknown heat transfer and shear rate profile in the screw.

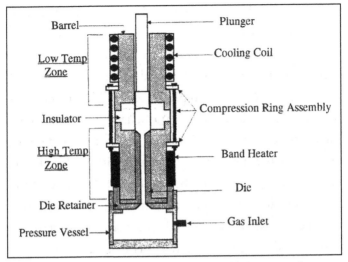

Extrusion rheometer showing low and high temperature zones and a pressurized exit to prevent flashing off of moisture to prevent protein morphology changes

We approached a company who sells commercial rheometers with this novel design and they were initially interested, but since we didn't have it patented, they were hesitant. I investigated patenting the design, but the university didn't have the funds to apply for one.

Why is the Strecker Name Related to Coffee and Chocolate Flavors?

One of the courses I took during my graduate studies was in food chemistry. It was important to understand what reactions were occurring in food during processing so that food scientists and engineers could predict and control what reactions took place during a high temperature process. During the course, the professor covered a chemical reaction called the Strecker Degradation Reaction. It was discovered in 1862 by a German chemist, Adolph Strecker. This reaction is responsible for the roasted, caramelized flavors in baked products, for flavors in chocolate, and for roasted coffee aromas. It has also been associated with malty flavors and in flavors found in cheese. The professor teaching the food chemistry course knew that my name was Strecker so when he covered this reaction in class, he asked me during the class if I was related in some way to this German chemist. I didn't know if I was related, so I went to the university library to research it. I also had a detailed family genealogy that went back to the 12th century, so I was sure I could find out if I was related to this chemist. I found his name in the family genealogy and cross referenced it with a document in the library about Who's Who in Chemistry which also listed Adolph Strecker's name. They were a match. So, was my interest in food engineering a coincidence? Maybe, maybe not! You decide…

The primary focus of my Ph.D. research endeavor was to uncover the reaction mechanisms and reaction rates occurring during extrusion of cereal feedstock. I knew that chemical engineers are trained and educated in reaction mechanisms and rates, so I wanted to get more background and education in this field, so I petitioned my advisor about getting my Ph.D. in chemical engineering but still have my research be in the agricultural engineering department under him as my advisor. Since my advisor, Dr. Cavalieri, in the agricultural engineering department was also a chemical engineer by background and was also a faculty of the chemical engineering department at WSU, I told him of my interest of getting my doctorate in chemical engineering. He agreed to it, so I changed my major to chemical engineering. I ended up getting a second master's degree in chemical engineering during the same time I was getting my doctorate since my advisor was funding my Ph.D. research from another grant and I was conducting research on that project as well as my Ph.D. research. I felt extremely fortunate to have Dr. Cavalieri as my adviser. He was an excellent researcher, mentor, and collaborator during my time of research under him. I enjoyed the research aspect of a university engineering program and even considered becoming a professor at a university, but as time went on and I saw the tenure process a new professor had to go through, along with the "publish or perish" environment of a university profession, and decided it wasn't for me. I finally completed my Ph.D. in chemical engineering in February 1994 after starting at Tacoma Community College twelve years earlier.

I was thirty-seven years old when I completed my college education. I never set out to go beyond getting a bachelor's degree and now I had two master's degrees and a doctorate all in engineering. I wasn't the smartest student or the brightest intellectually, but I was willing to work hard and never give up. So, take heart from my experience and go for whatever you think you want to do with your life, be flexible with your expectations, work hard, and don't let anyone tell you that you can't do it. It took a lot of time, effort, and work to get through all those years of college. In our "instant society" where many things are evaluated, and life decisions are made by how quick I can get it; this endeavor could seem like a daunting pursuit. I can honestly say that at many times it did seem daunting and unattainable, but by focusing on a class or subject at a time and doing the best I could, I eventually completed my education. By the time I completed graduate school my kids were in middle school and thought all dads went to school all their lives! My wife and kids were very patient with me and I give them a lot of credit for the big part they played in helping me complete my education with supporting me through all those years of school and keeping me grounded as an individual. I learned from them to not take myself too seriously, have fun along the way, value relationships above everything, and enjoy life outside of school. All these traits would help me tremendously in the coming years of working as an engineer in industry.

KELLOGG'S AND CEREAL ENGINEERING

Kellogg's Corn Flakes: "They're great!!"

My job at Kellogg's was not my first choice when I completed grad school and started looking for work. I had already received a tentative job offer at the Hanford nuclear site working at Westinghouse in their environmental remediation of hazardous chemicals project. I had interviewed with Westinghouse and was waiting for my final confirmation letter when I heard back from Kellogg's after an initial phone screening call and was invited for an on-site follow up interview. I decided to go to Kellogg's for the interview since I had not heard back from Westinghouse yet and I was interested in the food extrusion technology and opportunity that would be at Kellogg's. While I was at Kellogg's in Battle Creek, Michigan, I called the manager at Westinghouse one evening to find out where things were with my job offer. He gave me the bad news that though they were ready to give an offer and he had it in front of him, he couldn't hire me because Westinghouse had just lost their contract with the Department of Energy at Hanford. What a blow! I was looking forward to working at Hanford, I knew a lot of other former WSU students who worked there, and it was in the Pacific Northwest. As I looked out my hotel room in Battle Creek in the middle of winter with snow on the ground, I had this gnawing feeling in the pit of my stomach that what I was seeing out my hotel room window might be our new home if the interview at Kellogg's went well. The interview process at Kellogg's took two days. The first day was interviews with individual managers and the second day was giving a presentation of my graduate work to rather large audience of interested employees and interviewers. After the presentation I was given a tour of the facilities and cereal plant where breakfast cereal was made. It was fascinating to see a building the length of three football fields churning out over a million pounds of cereal per day! And that was only one building at one plant. Kellogg's had cereal plants all over the world. I left Battle Creek later in the day after the plant tour and had a feeling that this was going to be the place where I would start my profession in engineering. A week after returning home, I received a job offer from Kellogg's. Since it was the only job offer I had received and I had a family to support, it wasn't a difficult decision.

Kellogg's provided a generous relocation package

and moved us and all of our belongings from Pullman, Washington to Battle Creek, Michigan, provided temporary housing for us while we looked for a house, and paid for closing costs on a house once we found one we liked. It made the transition much easier and allowed us to focus on getting settled into our new surroundings. We had never lived outside of Washington state until moving to Michigan, so it was a big move for our family. We were amazed that at times the whole city and suburbs smelled like toasted cereal. Post was making their Blueberry Morning cereal at the time and you could smell the toasted blueberry smell all over the city! It sure was a more pleasant smell than the stinky pulp mills we grew up smelling in Everett, Washington.

Definition of Ph.D.: Push here Dummy!

I started at Kellogg's in April 1994. My first position at Kellogg's was in a product development group that was responsible for working on new and existing cereal products. I worked with the food scientists who were experimenting on new product ideas and tweaking existing products for either new product claims such as higher calcium levels or to compete better against existing competitor products. One of my first projects I worked on was developing a process for higher calcium levels in Product 19. Product 19 was originally introduced in 1967 to compete with General Mill's Total and it was finally discontinued in 2016, so it had a product life of almost fifty years! The cereal consisted of lightly sweetened flakes made of corn, oats, wheat, and rice, marketed as containing all required daily vitamins and iron. While I was at Kellogg's, there was a push to increase the calcium levels of Product 19 as well to compete with competitor products such as Total who were claiming higher calcium levels than Product 19. The challenge with increasing calcium in Product 19 was that it made it sticky and it would not go through the flaking process very well since it would stick to the flaking rollers and clog them up. Kellogg's had a quite impressive pilot plant where we did all our testing on new products and product improvements such as Product 19. The pilot plant had all the processing equipment that was used on a production line and enabled us to run tests and experiments without disrupting the production line. The pilot plant was where all the Product 19 product improvement with higher calcium levels was done. We spent months trying to achieve the calcium levels of Total but could never reach it because of the products stickiness issue. Product 19 consisted of four grains mentioned above, but Total only consisted of whole wheat grain, so that's why we believe they were able to formulate with a higher calcium load than we were because of the grains used and interactions with calcium. We were able to increase the calcium levels but never achieve the value of Total. Marketing put their spin on it and with our brand recognition, we did okay. I worked on a number of product improvement projects during my year in product development. I enjoyed the group I was working in and my manager was great. Kellogg's had a great corporate culture, and it was reflected in how they treated their employees. It was a fun work environment and challenging, interesting work. I ended up having a lot of interaction with marketing and found I really enjoyed working with them. It was a good way to learn about Kellogg's business and how they served and reached out to their customers. One funny story was when a batch of Fruit Loops was made with the wrong blue food coloring. There were several options and one of them was not good. It was not a food safety issue, but just how the body metabolized it. After this batch went to market customer service started receiving frantic calls from concerned mothers complaining that their baby's diapers were blue! The blue food coloring was just passing through and turning the poo blue!! It was comical in a sense since we knew there was no harm to the babies, but we felt bad for the frantic mothers who were having to deal with blue pampers. The mistake was found and corrected, no babies were harmed, and Kellogg's made sure that never happened again.

During my year in product development, I learned how Kellogg's cereals were made and produced. One cereal, in particular, was fascinating in how they made it and the process that was used. Corn Pops was made using a four-story vacuum chamber column where the hot extruded cereal was injected into this column and rapidly expanded to its final shape. It took a four-story column because that's how far it shot up into the column before losing enough velocity so when it hit the top it didn't just disintegrate from the impact. We were looking into simplifying the process by using an extruder but the product texture from an extruder was very different from the vacuum chamber process, so the old method stayed in place. Another cereal that was Kellogg's flagship product, Corn Flakes, had an interesting history of how it was developed. The flavoring was made by producing a wort similar to how a beer is made up until it is fermented. In fact, Kellogg's hired Anheuser Busch to develop the process for them. I saw the production facilities where the corn flake wort was made, and it did look like a beer brewery facility! Another production line that was fascinating to see and watch in action was the frosted Mini wheats. It's actually a very simple process where whole wheat berries are cooked and then run through a mill where it creates "strings" of whole wheat which are then lapped on top of each other to create the biscuits. In all these products and processes, there was a lot of engineering and development behind them that took years to complete. One of the first processes that I learned to operate in the pilot plant was a rotary cooker. It was a large cylindrical vessel that was heated and pressurized with steam. It was used to cook corn grits used in Corn Flakes and it was used for cooking grains for other products as well. The technician who was training me on how to operate the rotary cooker had been at Kellogg's for many years and was quite a character. We ended up working a lot together and he had a wealth of knowledge that I learned a lot from. When he found out I had a Ph.D. we were in the pilot plant doing something with one of the rotary cookers. He pointed to the start button and told me that it was a Ph.D. button: Push hear Dummy! We both had a good laugh. I think he liked me because I didn't take myself too seriously and could joke around with him at my expense. It was a lesson in humility. Be willing to learn from anyone because someone always has more experience than you.

Kellogg's History, Culture, and DNA

Corn Flakes was the first cereal that Kellogg's produced as a company. It was created by W.K. Kellogg in 1898 for his brother John Kellogg who ran a health spa, called a sanitarium in those days, who wanted a healthy food for his patients. In 1906 W.K. started the Battle Creek Toasted Corn Flake Company and in 1914 the company name was changed to Kellogg's. At one time there were over eighty cereal companies in Battle Creek[5]. By the time I arrived there were only three: Kellogg's, Post, and Ralston.

Kellogg's culture as I alluded to above was great from an employee viewpoint. They encouraged teamwork, employee development and education, a generous benefits package, and emphasis on work-life balance. The DNA of the company was based on business, marketing, and sales. Engineering was in support of these functions for the most part. Most of the innovation was in marketing and sales, though some occurred in engineering. Since the CEO and upper management were not engineers, it was not in their sights to promote engineering innovations. We had to "sell" an idea for a new technical process and equipment or new way to approach manufacturing. As I will go into more detail in the chapter on HP, HP's DNA is engineering. It was started by engineers, run by engineers, and engineering innovation was encouraged and promoted. This is what eventually drew me to pursue a job with HP, but at the time I didn't know as much as I do now about how different the DNA at Kellogg's was than HP's.

A Material Science Approach to Food Engineering

After a year in product development, I moved to the research and development (R&D) group to begin work on extrusion process development and innovation. Kellogg's wanted to utilize my food extrusion expertise from my Ph.D. research to expand how it was used for their business and products but placed me initially in product development to get a good overview of the company and how products are made and marketed. Any shaped cereal is usually produced using extruders which cook and form the shape all in one process. It can also be used to form pellets which are then run through a flaking mill to make flaked cereals.

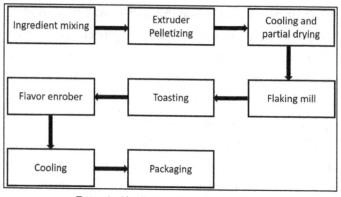

Extruded/pelletized/flaked breakfast
cereal process flow diagram

That's how Product 19 was made since it was a composite of four grains and an extruder did a great job of mixing those grains together and then pelletizing them in preparation of going through the flaking process. The first couple of months were spent visiting extruder machinery companies that Kellogg's used for the current production and getting to know who's who in the extruder industry. I also started networking with other companies and universities who were on the cutting edge of extrusion technology whether for food, plastics, or novel chemical processing techniques using extruders to mix specialty chemicals. I participated in a university food technology industry working group at Rutgers in New Jersey where they hosted annual meetings for leading food companies like Kellogg's. It was a good place to tap into scientific and engineering expertise at the university. One of the challenges at Kellogg's and, really, at any company using extrusion technology whether food, plastics, or chemicals, was how to scale up a process from a pilot plant scale to a large production scale process. Since food is a very complex biochemical system including proteins, carbohydrates, and many other constituents, it is very difficult to find one chemical reaction that can be used to scale the process up using dimensionless process parameters which is done for many chemical and plastic extrusion processes which have many less constituents and reactions to deal with.

M.Photografer/Shutterstock

Cereal extrusion process showing exit of extruder die plate which forms the shape of the cereal, in this case a round die plate hole shape

While at Kellogg's I was always looking for that holy grail for scale up. One area that I was able to provide some innovation was with predicting food expansion when exiting the extruder die. The die plate on the exit of the extruder is where the cereal shape is formed. The heated, moist cereal exiting the extruder flashes off the moisture in it and expands as a result in unpredictable ways. For instance, if you are trying to make a dinosaur shaped cereal and make a die shape exactly the dimensions that you would draw on a sheet of paper, it would expand all out of proportions. The extremities would become tiny and the main body of the dinosaur would look bloated. The areas of the die with more of the heated cereal would expand greater than the tiny areas where the head, legs, and tail were. So, the trick was to figure out how to do that since it took days to have each die plate precision machined and then tested to see if the correct product shape was attained. If the shape were not acceptable, a new die plate would have to be machined and tried again.

Example of various die plate designs
for producing shaped cereal

Most of the time it would be many iterations before an acceptable product shape was achieved. I became aware of a group at McMaster's University in Ontario Canada who were doing extruder die simulation work for plastics extrusion processes. Plastic extruders have the same issues except they are usually flashing off solvents, not water, but resulting in similar issues with final product shape and dimensions not being very predictable. They had developed a die flow simulation software package, ProfileCAD, that was available for sale and I went up to Ontario to visit them and see how it worked. It was really amazing the research and innovation they had done to come up with this modeling software. The material properties such as viscosity, density, heat transfer coefficients, moisture content, etc., and extruder processing parameters such as screw speed, extruder length, process temperatures, etc. could be entered into the model and it would show die shapes and predicted product shapes based on these inputs. I talked Kellogg's into purchasing a software package and testing it for our extruders and products. We brought it in house and began testing it to see if it would help us reduce die shape iterations. One thing that it showed us right away was that with the dinosaur shapes the extremities such as head and legs needed to be larger in proportion so that more cereal was flowing in those sections of the die when exiting the extruder. Since more material was flowing in the extremities, it expanded more and looked more proportional to an actual dinosaur shape. Once we were able to tweak the die shape with the software, we could then download the CAD design from the software and then machine the die with the new shape. We were able to achieve the correct product shape on the first try and not have to do any further die shape iterations. Success! It was a great win for us and greatly accelerated our process development and, ultimately, our time to market. This development had come about by using a material science approach to food engineering that I had learned during my Ph.D. research. Once the material properties of the cereal were known, then more accurate modeling could be done. It was very fulfilling to realize that my research in grad school could be applied to real world problems and to solve complex processes.

Kellogg's had a world-class analytical lab that rivaled any lab in either the food or chemical industry. They had chemists and food scientists utilizing the latest chemical and material property analysis to better understand the properties of food in order to predict incoming ingredient quality to final product quality and everything in between. I really enjoyed my job at Kellogg's and would most likely have still been there if it hadn't been in Michigan.

Throughout my second year at Kellogg's working in R&D, we were beginning to miss the Pacific NW and our families back there. I was torn between the great job I had at Kellogg's and the life outside of work in Michigan. There were some things we liked about the state of Michigan, but it didn't compare to the beautiful state of Washington. We were used to the extreme cold winters in Pullman but the extreme humid heat of Michigan during the summers was unbearable. We were used to the lower humidity summers of the Pacific NW where the Pacific Ocean acted like nature's air conditioner and we could usually be enjoying the outdoors all summer long. Not so in Michigan. When we woke up in a humid summer morning in Battle Creek and looked out the window, we could see the moisture in the air and just dreaded going outside. So, I started to look for jobs back in the Northwest. I had a former grad school colleague who went to work for HP's printer division right out of grad school, so I contacted him to see if there were any opportunities there. He put me in touch with some HP engineers in the San Diego printer division site. I had a phone interview with them, but nothing became of it. He then gave me a name of a manager at the Corvallis, Oregon printer division site who I started trading emails with over a couple of months' time in late fall of 1995 and eventually got a phone interview set up in early winter of 1996. The phone interview went well, and they invited me out to Corvallis site for an on-site interview in early April. I timed the interview so that I could utilize the long Easter weekend holiday that Kellogg's gave us to travel out so that no one at Kellogg's would suspect anything. My interview was scheduled for Monday, the day after Easter, and I was also taking Tuesday off to give me time to travel back and be back the office on Wednesday. I flew out of Kalamazoo, Michigan, on Easter with snow flurries and landed in Portland, Oregon with sunny skies and seventy degrees. Wow, what a difference! I got my rental car and drove to Corvallis with the windows open, drinking in the fresh, warm air and telling God, "Please, please let me have this job!". My interviews lasted all day Monday and the engineering team I was interviewing for was a great team. I liked the people I interviewed with and my wrap up interview was with the hiring manager. He and I hit it off and I felt that I had a good chance at the job. I left Corvallis that evening to drive back up to Portland where I would fly out of, and it was an hour and a half drive. Again, I told God, "I really would like to have this job!". I flew out of Portland the next morning and arrived home mid-day. I went back to work on Wednesday, and no one had a clue that I had flown out to the west coast for an interview. A week later I got a call from the hiring manager with a job offer. They were offering me twenty percent more than I was earning at Kellogg's. The food industry notoriously underpaid engineers and with the offer from HP it made it all that more obvious. Before the HP offer came in, I told my wife that I would accept any offer from HP even if it was the same salary I was making at Kellogg's. So, when the HP offer was twenty percent higher it was icing on the cake! I accepted it immediately and negotiated a start date for mid-June so we could wait until the kids were out of school for the summer. I told my manager at Kellogg's about the offer and asked if I could stay at Kellogg's until early June, two months from then. I wasn't sure they would want to keep me that long since I already had an offer, but my manager said that he wanted to keep me as long as he could and really didn't want to lose me. I liked my boss and we got along well, so I was sad in that respect. He asked me when I had the time to go out to Oregon for an interview and I told him that I did it over the long Easter weekend. He was pretty surprised when I told him that HP in Oregon had made me an offer, so that's why he asked.

We put our house on the market in May and had a full-priced offer within two days. The house sale closed, and we had the money in the bank before we left Michigan. It was nice to have that all taken care of before leaving town. HP was paying for all of our moving expenses, so we decided to drive from Michigan to Oregon and turn it into a mini vacation. We stopped in Chicago, went to the Mall of America in Minneapolis, visited my brother-in-law in Sioux Falls, South Dakota, stopped to see friends in Spokane, Washington, and went to Pullman to see friends before continuing to Corvallis, Oregon. It was a five-day drive across the country. We were all anticipating getting to our new home in Corvallis. My wife and kids had not seen Corvallis before we moved there so they were anxious to see where they were going to be living. HP provide temporary housing for us in an apartment while we searched for a new house. It felt good to be back on the west coast and in Oregon, within a few hour's drive to our family in Everett, Washington. I was also looking forward to starting my new job at HP's inkjet printer division in Corvallis, the site where inkjet had been invented a decade earlier.

HP AND INKJET ENGINEERING

HP's History, Culture, and DNA

Bill Hewlett and Dave Packard were both Stanford University electrical engineering graduates. HP (short for Hewlett Packard) was founded by Bill Hewlett and Dave Packard in 1939. Their first product was an audio oscillator and one of their first customers was Walt Disney. Disney used the oscillator to test audio equipment in twelve specially equipped theaters showing Fantasia in 1940. HP entered the computer market with the HP 2116A in 1966. Since the founders were engineers, the DNA of the company was engineering. They encouraged innovation from the beginning and allowed engineers to spend at least ten percent of their time on skunk works and new ideas. There was also an entrepreneurial culture, always looking for new ideas that could turn into products. Throughout my career at HP, I was able to be involved in a number of new product ideas and introductions. It was an exciting environment to be in as an engineer.

Manufacturing Process Engineering

I started at HP in June 1996 just ten days before my fortieth birthday. I didn't tell anyone at my new job that it was my birthday, especially since it was the big four oh! I wasn't the oldest person in my new group at HP, but I certainly wasn't the youngest either. The job I interviewed for at HP wasn't the one I ended up getting once I started there. Since there was a couple of month gap between when I got the offer and when I started, they had moved people around, so my new job was different. It was common to have that happen at HP, particularly with the rapidly growing inkjet business. The HP site was the size of a small city in both the number of employees and buildings on site. It was a one hundred-seventy-six-acre site with ten buildings with over two million square feet of office and manufacturing. It was the largest employer in Corvallis at the time and also HP's largest site for the inkjet business. The site had doubled in size over a five-year period driving housing prices through the roof by the time we arrived in 1996. The site was the inkjet cartridge research and development center along with high volume inkjet cartridge manufacturing for HP's printer division. My job was in the intermediate assembly process where the silicon die was bonded to the flex circuit of an inkjet cartridge.

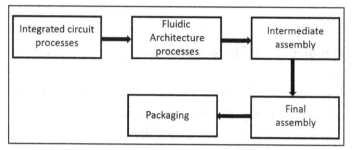

High-level inkjet cartridge manufacturing flow diagram

There were over sixty individual process steps in manufacturing an inkjet cartridge, from a silicon fab similar to ones used for making integrated circuits used for computer chips, to final assembly where all components of the inkjet cartridge were assembled, and ink filling occurred. HP was the market leader for inkjet printers and business in the mid 1990's was booming. They couldn't hire people or ramp up manufacturing lines fast enough to keep up with demand and were in danger of losing business if they couldn't keep up with demand. So, hiring an engineer from the food industry to work in high tech might seem like a surprise, but they were taking anyone they could find to help them with new manufacturing lines and developing manufacturing technologies to speed up cycle times and improve reliability, two things that continually plagued inkjet development. It was quite a change from working with large industrial extruders that could weigh several tons and produce thousands of pounds of cereal an hour to now be working with small inkjet cartridges that had nozzles smaller than a human hair! The difference between the scale of the equipment and manufacturing was staggering but fascinating beyond imagination. And my background on how the process interacts with material properties was exactly what HP needed for engineers working with inkjet manufacturing and process development, skills that were transferrable from one industry to another. I didn't realize that I would end up working at HP for over twenty-three years in the inkjet division.

My job in intermediate assembly was a manufacturing engineering position where I was responsible for a specific process used in the inkjet cartridge production. In intermediate assembly three components came from upstream processes: a sawn silicon wafer containing hundreds of silicon chips, or "die" as HP called them, a sheet of metal orifice plates that were fabricated in a precision metal plating process, and flex circuits which were made for us by an outside vendor. Intermediate assembly was responsible for attaching a metal orifice plate to a silicon die and then wire bond the flex circuit to the die to produce a tab head assembly (THA) that would then go on to final assembly downstream from us to be attached to the plastic inkjet cartridge body. The first step of assembling a THA in intermediate assembly was to singulate the metal orifice plates since there were hundreds of them per sheet and only one was needed per cartridge. I was responsible for the orifice sheet singulation process. The process used a machine which used blue sticky tape which had a pressure sensitive adhesive on one side that held the orifice sheet in place during singulation. The machine to do this was called a breaker tool since that's how it singulated the orifice plate by breaking the connecting tabs between all the orifice plates on a sheet. The breaker tool would utilize the material properties of the metal orifice sheet so that when deformed enough, the connecting tabs would snap apart and allow the subsequent pick-and-place tool to remove each orifice plate at a time and then align and attach them to a silicon die. The breaker tools had been in production for a few years and needed to be replaced since they were starting to break down frequently and were unreliable. So, my first project was to redesign the breaker tools. I worked together with a maintenance technician to come up with a better design. I let him have pretty much full reign on how he did it and he was really excited to be able to do it. He had a lot of great ideas and since I had been a technician before, I knew what they were capable of doing and how valuable they were to an engineering team. I saw too many engineers who put down technicians to their own detriment. I saw technicians as great assets to any engineer and that's how I was going to approach this project by letting the technician own the design and be the leader on it. I wasn't trying to get out of the work, but I saw that he was really good at mechanical design, much better than I was, so I let him be as involved as he wanted to be. Within weeks he had a new design and parts list for the new breaker tool and within a month we had a new and improved breaker tool on the production line working flawlessly. We immediately started work on another breaker tool since production was increasing and it would be good to have a backup one available. During the height of production, we were making millions of THAs a month in intermediate assembly. HP was great at making sure their engineers stayed current on technology developments in the industry for tooling and process development, so we frequently went to trade shows and conferences to keep up to date on developments. On one such trip to a large industry tradeshow in Anaheim, I saw a laser cutting tool that was used to cut metal and realized that this might be able to be used for the metal orifice singulation process. One of the issues we had with the breaker tool was causing bent orifice plates. The nozzle diameter on the orifice plates was shrinking and that resulted in thinner orifice plates which were more ductile than brittle when thicker and the breaker tool was reaching its limit. So, I had been keeping a look out for new technologies that could be used to singulate the orifice sheets and this laser cutting process looked very attractive since it would not bend the orifice plate when cutting them. The one thing I didn't know was if the laser would also cut the blue sticky tape when cutting the metal above it, which held the orifice sheet and needed to stay intact for the process to work. I decided to send some blue sticky tape samples to one laser vendor to test for us and the laser didn't damage it at all. The film was invisible to the laser beam at that wavelength, so that was the first hurdle that we passed. Further testing would need to be done to see if the metal being cut would damage the sticky tape from heating up during cutting. We tested it as well and found it did damage the sticky tape a little but not enough to melt all the way through. So, we put in a purchase order for the first laser cutting system. I was transitioning out of the intermediate assembly manufacturing position into an R&D group before the first laser system arrived. My replacement in the manufacturing group was the one who took over the project after I left. I did stay in touch with him to see how everything progressed and they eventually used the laser cutting process for all metal orifice plate singulation world-wide, so it was great to see it gain traction and be adopted. It enabled non-contact singulation which resulted in uniform, flat orifice plates which resulted in more consistent drop trajectory of the nozzles since bending caused ink drop trajectory issues due to the nozzles not always being orthogonal to the orifice plate plane.

Ergonomic Spinner Knob Startup Business

While working at HP full time, I got involved in a few startup businesses that I worked on after hours. One of them was the development of a patented forklift driving aid, called a spinner knob. A couple of friends of mine wanted to start a business selling a new and improved spinner knob that one of them had come up with. The one friend drove forklifts for a job at a distribution center and had this idea for a safer, more ergonomic knob design. If you've never heard of a spinner knob before, they are used on forklifts to aid the driver in turning the steering wheel more easily. They have also been used in cars and trucks over the years and are still available online. The traditional spinner knob (also sometimes called a suicide knob due to them breaking arms and hands during operation) are a knob attached to a steering wheel that a driver can hang on to and "spin" the steering wheel with. This knob spins since it is attached to the steering wheel with a clamp and has a bearing at the base of it that allows it to rotate freely. The new design idea for the spinner knob was to "flatten" the knob design so a driver would "palm" the spinner knob by placing their palm on the knob rotating flat surface instead of grasping a protruding knob with their hand.

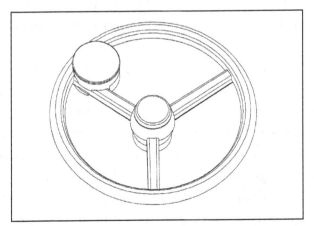

U.S. Patent 6,701,801 Flat profile spinner knob design as shown attached to a steering wheel. Note the low profile design.

It's a similar action to when a person uses their palm to turn a car steering wheel by placing the flat palm on the wheel and turning it instead of using a hand-over-hand turning action. The flat knob design was safer since no protruding knob stuck up above the steering wheel to smack a hand or fingers on. It was also more ergonomic since a driver didn't have to continually grasp a knob but keep their had in a more natural open position. My friends and I put together a limited liability company, LLC, and named it Innovative Industrial Products. The first thing we did was patent the new spinner knob design[x]. We worked with a patent attorney to write the patent and he also helped us in communicating with the US Patent Office agents. I initially recommended we not patent the design for several reasons. One reason was for the exorbitant cost of obtaining a patent. It cost us over $10,000 for the patent. The other reason was that we didn't have the resources to enforce the patent. If someone or company were to infringe on our patented design, we would have to take them to court to force them to cease and desist, all requiring expensive attorney and court costs, which we didn't have. So, I encouraged my partners that we should go to market without a patent. Since the design would likely be copied anyway, instead of court battles, we would get an edge by being out in the market first. If it got copied, we would still have a market share and most likely benefit for more market exposure even by the counterfeits. But my partners wanted the patent, so we went ahead and got one. We applied for and obtained a Small Business Administration (SBA) loan to help with the patent and product development costs. Once we had the patent, we started the design and manufacturing processes. We ended up using an injection molding process to manufacture the spinner knob which was all plastic construction with an over molded soft rubber layer on the flat spinner surface to aid in comfort and grip to a palm. After the spinner knob was completed, we went to Oregon State University engineering department to have a senior design class conduct ergonomic studies as a part of their senior design project. The ergonomic study compared our design with the traditional spinner knob design which a driver had to grasp instead of palming it. Their study confirmed that our flat spinner design was indeed more ergonomic than the original knob design. This was a great outcome for us, and we used it in our marketing materials to highlight its benefits to forklift drivers. We went to forklift manufacturers like Hyster and Toyota, two of the largest forklift companies at the time, to gauge their interest in the new spinner knob. Hyster was interested in testing it on their forklifts and used it at the R&D center in east Portland for testing and potential customer feedback. They received mixed reviews from their customers. Some loved the new design and others didn't. Toyota wasn't interested in testing it at all. We went to a forklift distributor for the west coast to see if they would carry them in their product line, but they weren't interested because of the low commissions their salespeople would get in selling them.

Their commission was much higher for selling a forklift than selling a spinner knob, so there was no incentive for selling them. We also went to places like Lowe's and Home Depot who use a lot of forklifts but could not get any traction with them either. After about five years of effort to make any reasonable sales and profit we decided to see if we could license the technology to a company. We had one after-market company who was interested, but they wanted a universal designed product that could fit on any model of forklifts. Our strategy had been to target the market leaders like Hyster and Toyota and make the spinner knobs custom fit for their steering wheels so that they didn't look like an add-on product but have an appearance of being an integral part of the steering wheel. The potential licensing company wasn't interested in that approach. They wanted a universal model. In the end, there was no licensing deal with the company, and we closed Innovative Industrial Products after five years. It was a fun business to be involved in, and I learned a lot about a new market I knew nothing about. I also liked the small, entrepreneurial aspects of a startup company.

Polymer Film Process Development

Now back to my day job at HP! I moved into an R&D group working on a new material that would be used to adhere the metal orifice plate to the silicon die. The current material was not robust enough for the inks used in the cartridges and there were field failures due to the orifice plate coming loose and leaking, sometimes detaching completely from the silicon die resulting in a complete failure of the inkjet cartridge. This was not a good customer experience! So, a large-scale project was started to investigate other materials that could be used to provide a more reliable, robust bond between the metal orifice plate and the silicon die. We talked with outside research groups, universities, and private research companies to see what material options were available or on the horizon that might be good candidates for us to try. We finally found a potential candidate, a polyimide polymer, that looked promising so we started a several year investigation to see how robust it was and what it would take to use it in a manufacturing process. Even if it held up against our aggressive inks, if it couldn't be easily adapted into our current manufacturing processes, then it might not be adopted. We found that it required a much higher bonding temperature than our current material and that needed to be evaluated extensively. We already knew that high temperature processes can impact all the materials in the silicon-orifice plate assembly and cause thermal expansion issues where stresses are built into the parts due to the materials expanding differently when heating it up and then, when it cools down, the materials contract differently, resulting in stresses. These built-in stresses can cause cracks for the ink to migrate into and possible reliability issues. So, a lot of work had to be done to investigate if it was possible to use a higher temperature, and if so, how to make it manufacturable. One of the challenges was developing fixtures to hold the silicon-orifice plate assembly while going through a linear high temperature furnace.

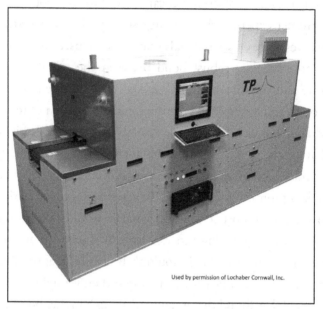

Used by permission of Lochaber Cornwall, Inc.

Linear high temperature curing furnace

As the assembly heated up it required a fixture to hold the assembly alignment in place, making the process much more complex. In the end, the polyimide material was not chosen because of the higher temperature bonding process and manufacturing complexities from requiring fixtures to hold the parts during processing. Though we continued to see field failures with the existing bonding material, we were able to improve it some by tweaking the existing material formulation and process parameters. HP had a new generation of printheads in the works that would eliminate the need for bonding metal orifice plates to silicon die altogether. It was a process that used lithographic processes used in integrated circuit fabs to fabricate both the silicon and the fluidic architecture all on one piece of silicon. So, the drive to find a new bonding material for printheads was going to be no longer needed and the material investigation was stopped.

Electronic Adhesive Process Development

I moved from this material R&D group into a material research group that was part of our supply chain organization who worked with our material suppliers. This group focused on the electronic adhesives that were used to bond the silicon die-orifice plate assembly (referred to as the printhead assembly) to the plastic print cartridge in final assembly.

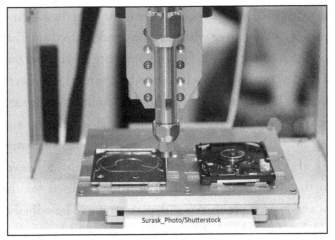

Surask_Photo/Shutterstock

Adhesive dispensing system

This had always been a weak link in print cartridge reliability since the ink in the cartridge would attack the adhesive bond between the silicon die and the plastic cartridge it was glued to. The adhesive was also the fluidic seal that kept the colored inks from mixing with each other. If one of these bond lines failed, the cartridge would either leak ink onto a customer or cause color mixing in the cartridge and result in poor image quality because the printed colors would have the wrong hue. So, a team was formed to evaluate what could be done to improve the adhesive bond reliability. With my manufacturing process background and experience with the previous group working on a bond line that needed to be fixed and new manufacturing processes developed for the new material, my role in this new group focused on process improvement and development. One of the first things we looked at was whether the manufacturing process currently used to cure the adhesive was curing the adhesive adequately enough or whether it was under-cured and that was the reason it failed. The adhesive cure process was one of the few processes which required a chemical reaction to occur. The engineers on the final assembly cure process were usually mechanical or electrical engineers and had no background in chemical reactions or chemistry. We also looked at the storage and use of the adhesives on the manufacturing line. The adhesive used for the process was a pre-mixed one-part epoxy. The adhesive supplier formulated the material to be mixed and then stored frozen so that no chemical reaction would occur until thawed to room temperature on the manufacturing line. Once the adhesive was thawed it had a specific use time before it was no longer usable due to becoming too viscous to be dispensed through a small syringe needle. Once it reached that point, it would be pulled off the dispense tool, and replaced with a fresh adhesive cartridge and syringe needle. As you can imagine, there was a lot of variability on how the storage and use on the manufacturing line was carried out. To determine how the adhesive storage and dispense process was being done in our manufacturing locations a group of us traveled to our manufacturing lines around the world. In one trip we traveled to all the HP world-wide production sites where our primary inkjet cartridge manufacturing sites were at the time. They all had final assembly lines which were using the one-part pre-mixed epoxy adhesive to attach the printhead to the cartridge body. At each site we provided training to the engineers, technicians, and operators on how to handle the epoxy adhesive and what was going on with the material chemistry during storage and use on the manufacturing line. They had no idea and, many times, didn't care what the material was doing as long as they could keep the manufacturing line running and reduce downtimes and line stoppages. We showed them the importance of understanding what the material changes were due to chemical reactions to prevent issues on the line in the future and ensure the adhesive was at an optimum condition for adequate curing. As the viscosity of the adhesive changed over time, the bond line that was dispensed would also change and could result in out of spec parts because the bond line was too wide or too tall. Once the printhead had been attached to the plastic cartridge body, it would go to the cure process step which was an oven that the parts traveled through to cure the epoxy adhesive. Optimum curing would only occur if the material were kept at the same conditions up-stream during storage and dispensing. If the material were left at room temperature too long it would already be partially cured, and the curing step would not produce the same material properties as when it was not partially cured yet. These material properties were important for ensuring the adhesive had maximum resistance to ink penetration and that the bond line dimensions were consistent and in spec.

Two-part Adhesive Process Development

Whenever a set of materials goes through a high temperature curing process, each material, whether an adhesive, silicon, metal orifice plate, or plastic in cartridge, has its own coefficient of thermal expansion (CTE) which determines how much it will expand and contract during a thermal cycle. The CTE of each material is different and the greater the difference will determine how much of a mismatch will exist between two materials and how that will contribute to built-in stress after the assembly has cooled down. These built-in stresses always exist in electronic assemblies such as computer chips but are particularly problematic for inkjet assemblies because of the ink. Ink is a good solvent for polymer adhesives, which is what all adhesives are made of. Examples of thermosetting adhesives are epoxy, cyanoacrylate, acrylic, and polyurethane chemistries. So, ink will attack the adhesive bond line over time and cause failure due to ink migration into a crack line caused by thermal expansion and the CTE mismatch between the two materials the adhesive is trying to bond together. There are two methods to reduce this thermal stress: 1) use materials with matching or close to matching CTE values, 2) reduce the curing temperature so the thermal impact is reduced, and less expansion and contraction occurs. For plastic inkjet cartridges, there is not too much that can be done with finding materials with matching CTEs. The plastic CTE is much different than the silicon CTE value, the two materials that an epoxy adhesive is trying to bond together, so when the epoxy is cured there is a resulting stress built into the part which the ink can then attack and degrade. We decided to start an investigation if a two-part epoxy could be used to lower the curing temperature and, thus, reduce the CTE stresses. A two-part epoxy has the resin and hardener separated versus the one-part pre-mixed epoxy that we currently used where the resin and hardener are already pre-mixed. With two-part epoxies, the resin-hardener ratios can be adjusted more easily and tuned for a given process. It also allows the epoxy to be cured at a lower temperature, even room temperature. If you have ever purchased a two-part epoxy from Home Depot to glue something together at home, you have usually let it cure, or "harden", at room temperature. The reason it can cure adequately at room temperature is that the hardener ratio is usually a lot greater than a pre-mixed one-part epoxy. A pre-mixed one-part epoxy hardener ratio is usually lower than a two-part epoxy so that it will not cure too fast when thawed out and requires a higher cure temperature to completely cure it. So, a two-part epoxy has a faster reaction rate due to the high hardener concentration. This results in requiring a lower curing temperature even to room temperature. We worked with our current adhesive suppliers to develop two-part epoxy samples that we could test on our assemblies to see if a lower cure temperature could be used and still maintain reliability and assembly specifications. The biggest challenge was not the material development but the process development for dispensing a two-part adhesive. Our current dispensing process for one-part pre-mixed adhesives used an auger value, also referred to as a positive displacement pump or rotary valve, to accurately dispense the adhesive onto the assembly. There was not an auger valve on the market for a two-part adhesive. I began a several year project on developing a two-part adhesive dispensing process that would work in our manufacturing line. One key insight that helped a lot with the dispense process development was that the auger valve was just a very small version of a single screw extruder that I had used in my research in grad school and at Kellogg's. The adhesive dispense auger valve had a 3 mm single auger screw in a shaft that "pumped" the adhesive out at very accurate flow rates. All the two-part mixers available at the time used static mixers attached to the end of a dual syringe which contained the hardener in one chamber and the resin in another chamber with different volumetric ratios. As the hardener and resin were pushed out of the chambers using air pressure, they flowed into the static mixer at the required ratios. As "static" implies, the static mixer was stationary and did not rotate or move like the auger valve. It did a good job of mixing, but it did not provide accurate flow rates. An auger valve, on the other hand, did both mixing and pumping at accurate flow rates. The engineers in the adhesive dispensing equipment industry were not familiar with extruders and didn't know that the auger valve was just a miniature version of a large-scale industrial extruder capable of mixing and pumping very well. With my extruder background, I saw the opportunity to use this auger valve as the single screw extruder it was and started testing it for mixing efficiency. I tested different mix ratios and it mixed all of them as if they were one-part adhesives. Now I just had to figure out how to design a new auger valve that had two inlets instead of the customary one inlet for one-part adhesives. I tested different inlet locations to see if the hardener needed to be injected earlier or later in the auger valve chamber. Testing showed that the resin and hardener could be injected in at the same location. I also tested the dual syringes that came in the correct volumetric chamber size so that when dispensed they were at the correct volumetric ratios. Since this was an industry standard for two-part dispensing it was decided to utilize this packaging. All that would need to be done is to design a method of connecting the dual syringe to the inlet of the auger valve. An inlet design on the auger was leveraged which used the current bayonet mounting of a static mixer to the end of the dual syringe. A patented design was obtained to achieve a way of connecting the dual syringe to the auger inlet using this bayonet method. This was one of seven patents[6-12] that were filed and obtained for the two-part auger valve assembly. A two-part epoxy dispensing system was designed and testing on our manufacturing lines which could plug into our existing one-part epoxy dispensing process. There was much interest in the two-part dispensing method we had developed by the adhesive dispensing industry. A friend of mine had worked for a company who specialized in auger valves for dispensing electronic adhesives for the high-tech industry. He was now working on his own as a consultant to companies who needed help with their dispensing systems. When he saw our design, he immediately asked if he could obtain a licensing agreement with HP to use this system for future clients. HP agreed to a licensing agreement and he began to work with a solar panel manufacturer who was trying to use two-part silicone adhesives in their process. Our two-part dispense system was exactly what they needed to accurately dispense two-part silicone adhesives in their process. Unfortunately, my friend contracted cancer and passed away before completing the project and I never heard how it eventually turned out. But it showed me that there were potentially many applications which could use a two-part auger valve system.

Two-Part Adhesive Dispensing Consulting Work

I was a consultant to a company which leveraged the two-part adhesive dispensing patents from HP. I was working with an engineer who used to work for an adhesive dispensing equipment company in southern California in which HP provided a lot of business and how I met this engineer before he left the company. He was the director of engineering and had a lot of expertise in adhesive dispensing systems and technology. He retired from the dispensing company and started his own consulting company focused on electronic adhesive dispensing business. He was interested in licensing the two-part adhesive dispensing patents and I worked with our HP lawyers to arrange the licensing deal. Once he received the licensing agreement, I worked part time with him as a consultant for two-part dispensing projects from time to time. One project was utilizing two-part silicone adhesives for use in a solar panel manufacturing assembly process. I also attended a trade show in Las Vegas and helped run the booth for the two-part dispensing equipment. It was during this time that my consultant friend contracted cancer and eventually succumbed to it, ending my involvement with the business. I was greatly saddened by his passing. He was a great guy to work with and the technology was something both of us were passionate about and wanting to see gain further inroads into high tech manufacturing processes.

Jetting Adhesives Using Inkjet Technology

On one of my visits to the southern California auger valve dispenser supplier to discuss auger valves since they were our primary supplier for them, they asked me if inkjet cartridges could be used for dispensing adhesives for applications which required very small drops. There was a lot of miniaturization of electronic parts and assemblies going on in the high-tech industry which required smaller and smaller adhesive bond lines. The current dispensing equipment was reaching the limit of how small a drop they could achieve and the idea of using the very small drops of an inkjet printhead looked very attractive to them. They told us of an application where the only method to achieve a small enough drop size was that the women on an assembly line in the Philippines were using their eyelashes. They would pull out an eyelash, dip it in the adhesive and then dab it on the part to get the drop size required. I asked what happened when they ran out of eyelashes and they said they would have to find other women to come in until the previous women's eyelashes regrew! Wow! That was an unsustainable process and not something HP would ever support, but if we could find a more humane and sustainable process for small drop dispensing using inkjet, then that would be a win for everyone. We began a multi-year investigation into using inkjet technology for dispensing adhesives.

Images Everyone/Shutterstock

Inkjet cartridge used for adhesive dispensing

This was many years before printed electronics began to emerge and be accepted as a technology for printing electronic materials such as LCD displays, printed circuit boards, and adhesives using inkjet technology. I approached management about pursuing this opportunity of using inkjet to dispense micro drops of adhesive along with one of our licensing attorneys at corporate headquarters in Palo Alto. Our attorney knew a retired CEO who was good at start-up companies, so we hired her as a consultant. I knew the former engineering manager from our auger valve dispensing supplier who was now working as a consultant and we hired him to be our technical lead. So, we now had a small team of four people who would spend the next two years investigating this opportunity. Two electronic adhesive materials we investigated were epoxies and acrylics. A couple of the challenges using thermal inkjet technology are the viscosity and thermal limitations. Inkjet ink is usually close to the viscosity of water. Electronic adhesives are much more viscous and are usually a paste. Inkjet uses heat to jet the ink by creating a bubble. This doesn't work for a paste adhesives. So, we went to our adhesive suppliers and asked them to formulate some epoxy and acrylic adhesives that were low enough in viscosity and not sensitive to short heating cycles. We actually took our inkjet dispenser with us to several of our adhesive suppliers so that we could test their formulations real time. On one visit that was for several days, the supplier was able to formulate an acrylic adhesive that dispensed and cured successfully. That was a critical step in our feasibility to show proof of concept to management and get continued support for the project. What would be required for successfully using inkjet for dispensing adhesives was not only an adhesive that could be used by inkjet but knowing how long an inkjet cartridge could dispense an adhesive before failing. Both epoxy and acrylic adhesives use solvents to formulate them, so we knew that they would most likely cause early failures in the inkjet cartridge due to the solvents attacking the polymer materials and adhesives use in manufacturing the inkjet cartridges themselves. How long they could dispense adhesives before failing was the biggest challenge we faced, though we knew from talking with prospective customers that since an inkjet could dispense very small drops, they would pay the premium for such a dispensing method even if a cartridge lasted only one day. That's how desperate some customers were for requiring small drop technology for dispensing. So, we went to work to determine how long an inkjet cartridge would work before failing. Before we could get too far though, the new business development group in our printing division that was funding our research decided to stop funding our project. This was a great disappointment to me and the team working on the project, but since it was out of our control, we documented our results and shelved the project. This is a good example, though, how HP was willing to take a risk and invest two years of time to investigate a potential technology and opportunity. It's what continued to make work interesting and engaging for me.

Adhesive Development for Permanent Printheads

In the early years of the new millennium, HP decided to make printheads that were permanent and that would last as long as the printer. The ink containers were replaceable, but the printheads were permanent. This meant that the adhesives to make the printhead for attaching the silicon to the cartridge needed to last as long as the printer. None of the epoxy paste adhesives that we used for this could meet this longer life criteria. To meet this challenge, the supply chain material development group was changed to focus primarily on how to develop a more robust and long-life adhesive for the die attach material. So, we went back to our suppliers and started asking them to come up with something that would have a longer life. What came out of those discussions was the idea of an epoxy film adhesive. Our adhesive suppliers knew how to do this, so the challenge was going to be for us to develop a completely different manufacturing process to enable using a film adhesive. We knew how to use one-part pre-mixed epoxy paste adhesives, but not epoxy film adhesives. That would require significant process development for how to place the film on a substrate, align it, and then cure it. In the end, it was the cure process step that was the most challenging. We found that with a film adhesive, voids would form between the substrate, film, and silicon die. What we eventually came up with was using a standard method used in the composite industry which used a pressure vessel (autoclave) to both heat and pressurize which reduced the voids.

Curing autoclave used for film adhesive

I worked with adhesive material and process development for over twelve years. It was fascinating and challenging work and the people inside and outside of HP who I got to work with were top notch engineers, chemists, and technologists. I was always amazed how much effort had gone into developing such a critical material and component of an inkjet cartridge and the host of people involved in the effort. I got to literally travel the world during those twelve years. I made most of my trips to our adhesive suppliers in Boston and Connecticut. I usually went to Boston two or three times a year. I had never been to Boston or Connecticut before, so it was fun to see these places and see so much of the early history of our country there. I had no idea when I started at HP that I would be doing this type of work, but it was a great experience that I would never forget. What I have found is that until you're working for company, you don't see all the technology and development required for bringing a new product to market. This was true for both inkjet cartridges and breakfast cereal. As I described above, the development of the cure process for film adhesives was not even understood until we got into the details of what was required. There were other methods tried before choosing the pressure cure process. Technology development is many times an iterative process using design of experiments and computer modeling to assist in the evaluation and decision-making process. Development also requires using engineering judgement and creatively looking at a problem or challenging design constraint to guide you as an engineer. This is something that is not taught but learned and it was one of the things I enjoyed most about engineering.

Advanced Printer Research and Development

My next position in HP was with an advanced printer research and development group where we looked at new methods of printing and new ideas for what to print. HP was the market leader for thermal inkjet printing, and they were always on the lookout for what next breakthrough or market disrupting technology would replace thermal inkjet printing. Other teams had done similar research for new printing methods prior, so our team started with their results, reviewed them, and decide on where to focus. After our review of possible new printing technologies, the team decided to pursue some ideas we had on new areas we could address with our current thermal inkjet technology as this would provide potential faster time to market. One area we investigated was printed security marks that we both covert (invisible) and overt (visible). HP has had a lot of issues with counterfeit printer cartridges where used empty cartridges are filled with non-HP ink but the packaging and boxes, they are sold to look like genuine HP cartridges and are sold at genuine HP cartridge pricing. The unwary customer doesn't know the difference until they get it home and start having issues with the print quality and cartridge life. HP loses a lot of money each year due to counterfeit cartridges. So, if a printed security mark could be printed on each printer cartridge box and simply scanning it or a visual mark that was easy to identify to determine whether it was a genuine HP cartridge, that would be a printing method not only valuable to HP but to any company selling products that were easy to counterfeit as well since many companies grapple with how to keep ahead of the counterfeiters.

A couple of covert printed marking technologies we investigate were invisible UV ink that fluoresced a bright blue when exposed to a UV light source and quantum dots which were also invisible when printed but fluoresced in other colors such as green and red when exposed to a UV light source. The added benefit of using quantum dots was the ability to tune them for both the amplitude of the signal and the spectrum. This provided a method to make each mark unique and change it easily to stay ahead of what counterfeiters might try to do to replicate it. At the time of our investigation, the main drawback of quantum dots was that they were made with cadmium, a toxic substance, so we did not pursue it past our initial assessments. The use of a UV ink, though, was looked at more closely and tested with our all-in-one printers where a sample could be printed and then scanned with the onboard scanner in the all-in-one printer with a special UV light source. The idea was that a print cartridge would have some UV components in the ink and a customer could print a sample and scan it to confirm it contained the fluorescent markers to confirm it was genuine HP ink. This all was probably more complicated than it really needed to be and that's the reason there were other people in the printer division looking at visible markings that could be added to the cartridge boxes that a customer could easily identify as being a genuine cartridge. Some of the printing technologies being used for paper currency, passports, and driver's licenses were also looked at. In the end, our packaging group took over the effort and were looking at the more easily implemented visible marking ideas that had come out of the investigation.

Another interesting side project that I worked on for about a year while in the advanced printer research group was investigating if fuel cell membrane catalyst could be jetted onto the membrane substrate using inkjet technology. It was in support of a government lab project with one of the large auto companies for developing a process for coating a fuel cell polymer electrolyte membrane (PEM) with the catalyst. The lab approached HP about helping them since they thought using inkjet might be a good process for doing it. So, I was selected for conducting the inkjet print testing of the material. It was basically a black ink with catalyst attached to the carbon black in the ink. It printed just like a black ink and there were no issues with the catalyst being affected by the thermal inkjet process. In the end, the auto company pulled out due to funding and market conditions at the time.

Environmental Life Cycle Assessment

This was a career move for me at HP. I had been in some facet of process or material development all my career up until this new job in a newly formed environmental assessment group. My former manager in the advanced printer group had made a move over to this new environmental group about a year earlier. HP was a leader in creating sustainable, environmentally produced products and we already had a large organization addressing the regulatory and recycling mandates for our industry. What this new environmental group was tasked with was to use environmental life cycle assessment, or LCA, for short, to evaluate the environmental impact from our products using a quantitative assessment that had been developed in the LCA methodology. My former manager contacted me to see if I would be interested in learning LCA and use it to quantify our printer environmental footprint including its carbon footprint, which is a subset of the overall environmental footprint. At first, I was not interested since my exposure within HP to environmental engineers were our product stewards. The product stewards were responsible for working with the product engineers to make sure our products met the regulatory mandates for energy use, recyclability, and banned materials. I wasn't very interested in becoming a regulatory expert or herding engineers into complying with regulatory requirements. As I talked with my former manager over the next couple of months, she was able to convince me to consider LCA work since it was more proactive, quantitative investigation into our printers. It was more of data analysis and engineering assessment than regulatory in nature and that piqued my interest. It was also a promotion which I had not had in the twelve years I had been at HP so far, so that was an added incentive. So, with some fear of the unknown, I decided to venture into something completely different and learn all about LCA.

LCA had its beginnings in the 1960s when concerns over limitations of raw materials and energy resources sparked interest in finding ways to account for energy use and to forecast future resource supplies and use. In 1969, researchers initiated an internal study for the Coca Cola company that laid the foundation for the current methods of life cycle inventory analysis in the United States. In a comparison of different beverage containers to determine which container had the lowest releases to the environment and least affected the supply of natural resources, this study quantified the raw materials and fuels used and the environmental loadings from the manufacturing processes for each container. Other companies in both the United States and Europe performed similar comparative life cycle inventory analyses in the early 1970's. In 1991, concerns over the inappropriate use of LCAs to make broad marketing claims made by product manufacturers resulted in a statement issued by eleven State Attorneys General in the USA denouncing the use of LCA results to promote products until uniform methods for conducting such assessments are developed and a consensus reached on how this type of environmental comparison can be advertised non-deceptively. This action, along with pressure from other environmental organizations to standardize LCA methodology, led to the development of the LCA standards in the International Standards Organization (ISO) 14000 series (1997 through 2002). Several LCA software products came out in the 1990's. SimaPro was developed by PRe Sustainability and became the most popular product. Another one, GaBi, developed by a German company, Sphera, is a competitor to SimaPro. I ended up using SimaPro for the LCA work I did for HP over a four-year period. I worked with four other engineers and chemists who also were in this new LCA group. We had all come from a manufacturing background and were very familiar with the processes that were used to manufacture an inkjet cartridge and a printer. We understood how each separate manufacturing process used energy, mostly in terms of electricity, which became an entry in the life cycle assessment. LCA Life cycle impacts cover all the phases of the development, production, use, and disposal of a product. Since we were familiar with the production it was intuitive how to approach it but LCA provided a solid framework of methods for gathering data to conduct an assessment. One thing we realized is that the print cartridge and printer bill of materials, or BOM, were lacking pertinent data to conduct an LCA. An LCA requires a list of the specific materials used to produce a product and the mass of each material used. Our internal BOMs did not account for the exact material used or the mass of each part. It typically had a part number, part description such as stepper motor or plastic paper tray, and quantity. For an LCA, the plastic paper tray, for example, would need to state what type of plastic it is made of such as polypropylene (PP), or acrylonitrile butadiene styrene (ABS). Each plastic has a different formulation and process, so its type is required to account for exactly what is being used. For the stepper motor, there are many subcomponents that needed to be accounted for such as stator, the copper wire windings, the magnets on the steel shaft, the aluminum body, etc., etc. Each component needs to be accounted for and determined how much energy it took to make it, and the environmental impact of each component. So, we had to hire an outside company to conduct a product tear down of the printers and cartridges we wanted to do an LCA on so we could get a complete list of components, materials, and mass for each one, down to the screws and glue used to assemble it. LCA also accounts for the use phase of a product, that is, how is the product used and what does it consume when being used. Printers use paper, ink cartridges, and electricity when a customer is printing with it. So, an LCA needs to account for all these as well to assess its environmental impact. For our printers we had an idea how much paper and ink cartridges were used and a rough estimate of energy use. One of the LCA studies I was involved in was for the determining the impact of printing books using an offset lithography press versus using an inkjet press. The standard process for printing trade paperback books is an offset press. We wanted to find out if there was a benefit for using an inkjet press. The study determined that an inkjet press has a thirty percent reduced environmental impact compared to an offset press due to being able to print on demand. An offset press is optimum for long runs, meaning thousands of books per run. An inkjet press can print hundreds of books and still be economical since it doesn't require lithographic plates for each run. So, an offset press usually prints thirty percent more books than are sold due to the limitation of requiring long runs. They overprint to make sure they have enough to meet market demands since they don't know ahead of time how many books will sell. This is where the environmental impact is reduced by an inkjet press by eliminating waste by thirty percent from unused books. As far as the overall environmental impact of an inkjet press in general, the paper use is the biggest impact since it uses a lot of paper. The next greatest impact is the energy use from the drive motors and dryer heaters. So, for a large inkjet press, the use phase is the greatest impact compared to the press materials and manufacturing, even though the large presses can weigh tons. For desktop printers, the greatest impact is the production and bill of materials, just the opposite of the larger inkjet presses, since it uses so little paper and energy to print. So, LCA was found to be a good way to quantify these differences depending on which printer and use conditions were considered. Another study was done which compared reading a book on an e-reader like a tablet or Kindle versus reading a book printed on an inkjet press. There ended up being a tradeoff curve where the more books which were read, the lower environmental impact would be reading the printed version. The greatest impact from using an e-reader was for the energy used to power the internet where the book was either downloaded from the internet or read from a cloud location without downloading it. Either way, the energy usage to power the internet for reading a book on an e-reader was greater than what we expected. We discovered that the server farms, the large facilities that companies like Apple, Google, and Facebook use, can have thousands of computer servers per building to support their internet service and can use over one hundred megawatts per year per site. This is enough energy to power around 80,000 homes assuming the average U.S. monthly energy usage is 877 kWh based on 2001 Energy Information Administration (EIA). So, from an environmental impact, reading a book are browsing the internet is not for free, it has an impact, and it can add up the more we use it. Another thing to think about is that some of the largest server farms are in states like North Carolina that have very cheap coal-fired power plants which have some of the worst impacts of any power source. One industry article called it "dirty data"!

I also got involved with one of my colleagues in developing an environmental footprint calculator that we provided our product engineers to help them in designing new printer products. It was an easy-to-use spreadsheet where the materials and mass could be entered in and it had look up tables that automatically calculated the impact for the user. One thing that the product engineers used it for was doing quick comparisons between material options and showing them real time how one material was better than another one. It helped them design better printers with better parts for both the environment and for product quality.

Another activity that I got involved in was with an ISO Standards working group who were leading the effort on developing a standard for calculating the carbon footprint of printers. I joined the working group to represent HP at the meetings since we were one of the largest inkjet printing companies in the world. It was very interesting and challenging to work with a group of people from around the world who all had their own agendas to push and represent, HP included. I worked in the ISO Standard group for over two years and attended meetings twice a year. I traveled to Berlin twice and to Sao Paulo, Brazil once. I learned a lot about how to be more diplomatic but still stand up for what I felt was critical and needed to be in the printer carbon footprint standard. The standard was for all printers whether an offset press for printing books and magazine, a flatbed press for printing large signage, or an inkjet web press for printing brochures and books. It was amazing to see how slow the process took since there were so many aspects and printer applications represented. Many hours were spent debating the minutiae and points of contention. Sometimes it was frustrating and maddening, but most of the time it was great to be a part of a group making a difference and influencing global decisions. On my trip to Sao Paulo, I arranged to meet with International Paper's research center just north of the city to see how they were using tree plantations for sustainable paper making. They had thousands of acres of eucalyptus trees which were used for hardwood in papermaking. The pulp for making paper is made up of both softwood (spruce, pine, fir, hemlock) and hardwood (eucalyptus, aspen, birch). Eucalyptus is regarded as the ideal fiber for printing and writing paper. Its wood is made up of short fibers, meaning a high number of fibers per unit weight. This provides paper with an excellent porosity, high opacity, and good formation. They could plant and harvest the trees in a five-year cycle. I was able to go to one of their plantations and see the process of harvesting. The stump is left in the ground and with the warm, humid climate that stump will completely decompose within five years. These tree plantations prevented old growth trees from being cut down and deforestation in Brazil. It was a success and showed how renewable paper is becoming with these types of operations.

Product Footprint Startup Business

I saw an opportunity with my experience in conducting LCAs that product teardowns were an area where I could add some value and be a nice business to run. So, I started a sole proprietor LLC company called, Product Footprint, where I provided product teardown data for any product a company needed it for in conducting an LCA. With my contacts in the LCA industry where I knew most of the big players who were conducting LCAs, I let them know of my services and started to develop a startup business in LCA product teardowns. Industry at the time was moving to encourage products to have an environmental product declaration in which a product category rule was used to define how a product in a given category was assessed for its environmental impact. LCA was the method used in determining the environmental impact based on the category rules. It was anticipated that there was going to be a big surge in the number of LCAs that were going to be needed to meet this regulatory demand. This never materialized because a new government administration came into office which wanted to reduce regulatory demands on industry and moved to eliminate this regulation. So, I only conducted a few product teardowns for various companies and then things dried up. I still get an occasional request for a product teardown, but not enough to make a living from. Again, this was all the while I was still working full time at HP. As you can see, in a career in engineering, you will see all kinds of opportunities for startup businesses and companies.

Material Regulatory Program Manager

After working for over four years in the LCA team, I was moved to a material regulatory position because some reorganization was occurring where they needed to reduce the headcount working on LCAs. I was sad to leave the group since we had accomplished so much is a short amount of time and it was satisfying to see the impact we were having inside and outside of HP.

My role in the material regulatory group was to track the materials used in our consumer inkjet printers and make sure we were staying on top of all the materials that were either banned, planning to be more heavily regulated, or under consideration by the external regulatory agencies such as the EPA. I had to make sure we were not going to use a material if it was already banned or have roadmap in place on how to replace a material if it was going to be banned in the future. There were hundreds of materials to keep track of and hundreds of regulations to be aware of. It wasn't the most favorite job I had at HP and I started looking for another job as soon as I could. Within a year's time I had found an application engineering position in our Specialty Printing Systems organization. It was a more customer facing job and I was going back into a more regular engineering role.

Specialty Printing Systems (SPS) Application Engineer

I had worked with SPS during the jetting adhesives project years before and was familiar with the organization so when I had a chance to apply for the application engineer position, I was excited. SPS is a small organization within HP which focuses on selling existing HP printing technology to original equipment manufacturers (OEMs) so they can develop their own printers and systems using our technology. SPS has its own marketing, sales, engineering, and supply chain to support this unique business. It really felt like a small company within a large one and had an entrepreneurial feeling and vibe to it. The organization was spread out over three west coast sites in Vancouver, WA, Corvallis, OR, and San Diego, CA. When I joined SPS in Vancouver, there were only three of us in SPS at the Vancouver site. By the time I left HP six years later there were over fifteen employees in SPS at the site.

The application engineer at the Vancouver, WA site where I was located now was moving on to a new job and so his position was open. I applied and interviewed for the position and was hired. It would be my last position in HP until I retired six years later. SPS works with OEM customers who are making their own printing systems using HP printers as their platform. We had several consumer and business printers that we had stripped down, usually removing the paper path for office paper, since their applications were many times not using paper at all. We had customers using our printers for printing passports, printing labels on DVDs, addressing mail, making labels, printing designs on bags and boxes, and many other applications.

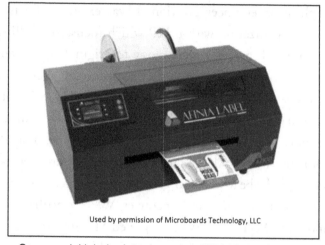

Used by permission of Microboards Technology, LLC

Commercial label printer based on HP inkjet technology

We also had a large business where customers bought only the print cartridges and then would design their own printing systems to use these cartridges. In fact, this part of the business was larger than the customers who bought an entire printer. There were five application engineers worldwide working for SPS. We had two for the Americas (North and South America) and I was one of them, two for Europe, and one for Asia Pacific. We were the primary technical facing person for our customers. If they needed help with their integration and development, we would assist them. If they later had issues with our printers, then we would also assist them. We worked closely with our sales team in vetting potential new customers to determine if they had the technical expertise to develop their own printing system. Though we could assist a customer during their development phase, they were responsible for all the mechanical, electrical, and software design. We would assist them if there were any firmware modifications required since that is one area that we controlled and did not allow a customer to modify or develop. I ended up learning how to modify a printer's firmware by using a scripting language HP had developed so non-firmware engineers could make modifications. I also learned how to customize the Microsoft Window's printer user interface (UI) in the Printing Preferences section in the Devices and Printers window of the Control Panel. This UI is where the page layout can be specified for portrait or landscape orientation, where the paper quality can be set, and where printing shortcuts can be specified. Our OEM customers want to have their company logo and printer name in this UI, not HP's logo and printer name. They also wanted to customize the UI for changing tab names and tab content. We provided them with documentation on how to make a customized UI for their printer, but I ended up helping many of them since there are so many nuances to how these are customized. I didn't have a software background, so I had to learn a lot of this on my own. It was a steep learning curve, but I eventually figured it out, and documented all of this into application notes that we could provide our customers to speed up their development time.

Most of my day-to-day work as an application engineer was working with existing customers in resolving problems they had with our printers or print cartridges. My favorite activity, though, was working with the sales group on vetting new or potential customers. We would either travel to a potential customer site to meet with them or sometimes they would come to one of our facilities on the west coast either in Vancouver, WA, Corvallis, OR, or San Diego, CA. We also attended various industry trade shows such as the packaging show in Las Vegas or a label tradeshow in Chicago where some of our existing customers and potential customers would be attending. It was a great place to gather information and data on what our competitors were up to and to see what trends were occurring in that industry and what we could do to address those trends. One industry trend that we were noticing was in printed electronics. This was getting back to my project of jetting adhesives a dozen years earlier. Piezo inkjet technology was the dominant printing technology that was being used in printed electronics because piezo inkjet was better at printing higher viscosity fluids and not using heat to jet a material used in printed electronic applications. Piezo printheads use an electrical actuated piezo material that moves mechanically versus a thermal inkjet printhead which uses heat to boil a fluid and jets a fluid from bubble formation forcing the fluid out of a nozzle. Most printed electronic materials are sensitive to high heat, so piezo inkjet is the primary reason it is used instead of thermal inkjet. Some printed electronic applications are using thermal inkjet printheads to jet materials such as dielectric coatings for multilayer circuit boards and primer coatings for batteries used in automobiles. I still think there are adhesive applications for using thermal inkjet such as miniature assemblies and precision coatings. SPS was not able to find potential customers in this area at the time we were investigating it in 2017, but I firmly believe that at some point, there will be opportunities in this growing field. One thing I learned from the adhesive jetting investigation twelve years earlier is that if a customer needed very small adhesive drops, they would gladly use a thermal inkjet cartridge even if it only worked for a few hours since it was an enabling a process to achieve the small drop sizes they required.

One of my favorite projects in SPS occurred in 2019 during my last year at HP before retiring. A large, national consumer products company had a unique cleaning product that they wanted to print images on to enhance the look of it. They approached SPS to see if we could test some inks they were using our inkjet cartridges. So, they sent us hundreds of samples and different colored inks along with image files we could use to print the shapes and text they were interested in using. I was heading up project for printing the samples and testing them to see how durable the ink was on the product. Our Corvallis, OR site had the most expertise with the print cartridges and printing systems to use these cartridges, so I set up the printing project with them. They had a printing test bed that could be customized to print on almost any size or shape of material. A standard printer would not be able to handle a large product which was twenty-five millimeters thick since the printhead was only within a few millimeters of the print zone. The printing system in

Corvallis could easily accommodate the thicker samples, so I arranged to have them all printed on their printer. For the initial print test, I traveled to Corvallis, about a two-hour drive from the Vancouver site. The technicians in Corvallis did a great job of configuring the printer to handle the image files I sent to them so that they could print on the unique size and shape of the products. The initial tests worked great and it was confirmed we would be able to print all the samples using that test bed setup. We had the several hundred print samples completed within a couple of weeks and then I tested them for durability, mostly water fastness, so a customer wouldn't get ink all over their hands using them. The inks that were sent to us were solvent based inks, not aqueous ink typically used for thermal inkjet applications. Fortunately, SPS had developed solvent tolerant cartridges and our existing solvent cartridge business was booming. We used the solvent tolerant cartridges for this testing, and they performed well. This large consumer products company was excited to see the samples we sent to them and they were in the process of sending those samples out to their customer base to gauge interest and potential business. As of the end of 2019, there was still no confirmation on whether this was going to be pursued, but it was a good example of the kind of opportunities SPS looks for.

Another area that SPS was involved in was bioprinting. They had developed a printer that is used by pharmaceutical companies for prescreening active ingredients in new product formulations. The typical approach for ingredient selection was to use a manual hand micropipette where a researcher must screen thousands of candidates using this pipette that is operated by hand. It is a big ergonomic problem in research labs. The bioprinter developed by SPS does this all by using inkjet printing, thus, automating the process, preventing ergonomic injuries, and increasing accuracy and productivity. I had an opportunity to give a demonstration of the bioprinter to our CEO at the time, Dion Weisler, in Palo Alto at an internal company product show where all the different printing groups in the division were participating by showing off their new printers and printer applications. It was a highlight of my career at HP to be able to speak one on one with our CEO. What impressed me about Dion, was that he was just like one of the guys, no ego, no pretenses, he just wanted to see how the bioprinter worked and showed a genuine interest in what I had to say. In all my years at HP he was the only CEO that I met personally.

Leaving HP

After a great career at HP of over twenty-three years I decided to retire at the end of 2019. I never thought I would make it this long since so much restructuring and global workforce reductions had occurred over the span of my career. I was fortunate to have the opportunity of a lifetime to work for such a great company.

I will miss the great people I had the privilege of working with, the products and technology I was part of in developing with other talented people, and a company that provided the opportunity to develop as an engineer and as a fellow human being. One of the things that made me want to stay at HP was the ability to always improve myself and develop new skills, the ability to move around to other jobs and learn new things and being able to work and learn from some very talented and top-shelf people! These are all great qualities to have in any company you work for, and I encourage you to look for these in your career path when considering which companies you want to work at. Remember, good relationships with your coworkers are most important. It's not how much you know but how much you care that you will be remembered by. Of all the things I miss about working at HP, the lasting relationships that were developed are at the top. Yes, the innovation, technology, and new products that were developed are right up there too, but they aren't what I miss the most. Work at developing good relationships and networks with people and you will reap rich dividends over your career.

I'm excited about the next phase of my life and this book is part of what I see in the new chapter of what I'll be doing. I'm going to explore more of my creative side in writing and music. It's an exciting journey I'm on and I hope yours is as well!

WHAT I HAVE LEARNED AS AN ENGINEER

Company Culture and DNA

As I explained above, the company culture at Kellogg's and HP were very similar for the employee's welfare, morale, and development. Company DNA, or how a company is run, from an engineering perspective, was very different at Kellogg's and HP. Kellogg's executives and upper management all had marketing, sales, or business degrees so their emphasis was focused on these areas. They had a large engineering staff and R&D organization, but it was mainly in support of the strategy passed down from marketing and sales. There was innovation but it was primarily in marketing and sales, not in engineering. HP, on the other hand, was started by two electrical engineers from Stanford University and the DNA of the company was based on engineers. So, the CEOs and upper management were engineers, and the company strategy and focus were on engineering, not marketing and sales, though they had those in the organization. All innovation and products were based on engineering decisions. The joke at HP was if we were selling sushi, it would be called "cold dead fish"! Engineers reigned at HP and the culture and DNA was all about engineering. HP has over 37,000 patents[13] which shows how much they invested in innovation and technology. I don't know how many patents Kellogg's has but I know it's not at this level. I knew that HP would be more of an engineering company than Kellogg's so that was one of my primary reasons for making the move to HP. So, when you're considering a company to work at be sure to check out the culture and DNA before making a decision. It can impact your career in a big way.

Networking throughout your career

My first job as an engineer resulted from networking. I was a member of AIChE, American Institute of Chemical Engineers, and I purchased their membership directory which had national listings of all the AIChE members, where they worked, and contact information. I used that extensively in my job searches right out of grad school and that's how I got my job at Kellogg's. I cold called a chemical engineer at Kellogg's using the contact information in the membership directory. When I introduced myself as a fellow AIChE member, he was more than happy to talk about opportunities at Kellogg's and provided other contacts at Kellogg's to talk to, which ultimately lead to a job offer. I had called other companies before calling Kellogg's and found that all the engineers at each company were very happy to talk with me once they found out I was a fellow AIChE member, so using your engineering membership is a great way to network when looking for a new or different job.

After I was at Kellogg's and started looking for my next job a couple of years later, I contacted a former classmate at WSU who worked at HP and used my college classmate network to get my foot in the door.

Once I was at both Kellogg's and HP, I developed internal networks of colleagues and contacts within each company to network with when looking to move laterally or up within each company. My first job at Kellogg's was in product development, but I really wanted to be in research and development, R&D. I let my manager know of my desire to be in R&D and he helped me by providing contacts in R&D. The same thing happened at HP where I had eight different positions during my career there and I used my extensive internal network to move into each of those positions.

Creativity is just as important as analysis

Some of my most important contributions came from being creative in my approach to a problem at hand or during development. I have covered two things I did above but will reiterate them again to prove my point. My first one was when I was in the R&D group at Kellogg's working on how to make the extrusion die plate design more predictive instead of the then current try-and-retry method. I leveraged technology from a different industry, plastic extrusion, and adapted it to food extrusion. I had learned during my grad school research on food extrusion that a lot of prior extrusion research and development done by the plastics and chemical industry was very applicable to food extrusion, and, in particular, extrusion die flow modeling. I didn't know about the die flow issues the food industry was having when I was in grad school, but once I was at Kellogg's it became apparent and I looked to the plastic extrusion research articles to see what I could find. That's when I found the McMaster's University research papers on the extruder die flow modeling software they had developed and had the "aha" moment that this just might work for food extruder die flow modeling as well. And as I shared more in depth above, it provided the tools we needed to more intelligently design an extruder die for shaped cereal.

The second one was when I was conducting two-part adhesive process development at HP and realized that the positive displacement auger valve was a single screw extruder at a very small scale which could be used to efficiently mix and pump an adhesive at very small flow rates for use in electronic assemblies for inkjet printheads. This resulted in seven patents with my name on it and a process that could be used to facilitate a potentially lower cure temperature for epoxy adhesives and lower built-in stresses in our assemblies. Again, it was making a connection between what one industry was doing with extrusion and what a completely different industry was using at a micro level and didn't even realize it was an extruder.

These two examples are ones that show creativity in making connections between industry processing methods and adapting them for other application. There are many other examples of creativity such as an engineer who designs a bridge or skyscraper or a car, or one who designs computer software code to make it user friendly such as the Windows or Apple icon-based software. By saying creative, what I am not saying is that it's superior to analysis. It's just part of the total approach to engineering. Analysis is always needed even after the creative part is done. I still had to do a lot of testing of the die flow software and positive displacement auger valve to verify that they worked for the applications, which required a lot of data and analysis, but I would have never arrived at that analysis for those ideas if I had not first been creative.

Inspiration and breakthroughs come on days off

Albert Einstein said that his greatest breakthroughs came when he was out on a lake in his sailboat. Sometimes, you must just walk away from a problem or technical challenge and think about something else. Your subconscious will still be noodling on it, but you will be thinking of sailing, going on a walk, or whatever pass time you like to do to relax. I have seen it happen on a weekend and suddenly, the issue I was grappling with at work would pop into my consciousness and I'd have an "aha" moment. I don't have these experience all of the time, but I have had them. What I have learned from them is that it is good to spend concentrated time on the problem, analysis, or research, but when you hit a roadblock and you aren't making any progress, take a break.

People skills are more valuable than technical skills

Engineers are not usually associated with professionals who excel in people skills. Rather, they are known for their technical, scientific, and analytical skills for design, development, and problem solving. I have seen over the years, though, that the ones who do excel with people skills are the ones who usually are more successful. People skills are things like being a good listener, showing empathy, showing others how much you care, not how much you know, being a good communicator, relating well with others, and willing to work together for the common good. Most engineers are good at the typical engineering skills so we're pretty much all on equal footing here. I know, we all have experiences with an engineer who is technically savvy and a child prodigy, but for the most part all engineers are trained to have about the same level of technical abilities. So, how do we differentiate ourselves? By developing good people skills. Our managers are aware of those who are team players and willing to get along with others and that makes them happy and look good to their management. Managers don't like to have to always be putting out fires that their engineers cause. No human likes that! So, when a manager has engineers who are easy to get along with, are willing to work to the common good, and actually have a personality, that goes a long way in advancing your own career. The best career advice I can give you is to invest in becoming better in your people skills and continue to learn new skills as an engineer. I will talk more about this below.

Don't be afraid of using engineering judgement

First, what is engineering judgement? Glad you asked. One definition is: "the ability to recognize and/or predict, through a combination of intuition, insight and experience, the probable outcome of an analysis, design or process." Some people have great intuition about mechanics for example because they tinkered with fixing cars growing up. So, they would have an intuition on how much torque a bolt could take before stripping or breaking it. If a person doesn't have this experience, then it will be difficult to make an engineering judgement on bolt size for instance. Intuition and insight can only come with depth and breadth of understanding and experience of a subject matter of which judgement is expected. I would not expect a junior engineer to have a lot of engineering judgement without prior experience of a subject matter. It only comes with experience. I used engineering judgement for using an auger valve for mixing a two-part adhesive. I knew from experience what an extruder was capable of mixing so that when I saw the auger valve, I could use my judgement and predict that it would mix these materials. Testing confirmed that judgement, but if I had not had that prior experience with extruders, it is likely I would not have been able to see the connection.

Learn something new, try something different

One of the best ways to grow in your career as an engineer is to keep learning new things. Every job I had at HP, which were seven different positions over my twenty-three-year career there, I had to learn something new, sometimes many new things. When I started in HP as a manufacturing process engineer, I had to learn a completely new industry and how an inkjet cartridge was designed and manufactured. In the polymer film material and process development job I had to learn about a new polymer film I had no experience with and how to process it at higher curing temperatures than we had ever experienced. In the electronic adhesive's material and process development job I had to learn about how epoxy materials are stored and used in inkjet manufacturing, how to cure them, what material properties are important during process development, how one-part and two-part epoxies are used and characterized, how to develop a completely new process for dispensing two-part epoxies, and how to jet an adhesive using an inkjet cartridge. In the film adhesive material and process development for permanent printheads a new process had to be developed for curing the film adhesive. In the advance printer research group, I learned about security marks and how they are used. I had to learn how to use industrial prototype printers to print novel materials to test them as possible candidates for covert security marks. All these positions up to this point had a similar thread to them about material and process engineering. The next few positions would be the biggest departures from that background I had developed in material and process engineering. In the LCA position I had to learn about environmental engineering and what life cycle assessment meant in that context. Since I had no background in environmental engineering, it was a steep learning curve for the first year or two. I also had to learn about how our printers functioned. Up until this position, my focus had been on inkjet cartridge manufacturing, not printer manufacturing. I knew very little about how a printer worked from an engineering perspective. The next position as a material regulatory engineer, was part of the environmental engineering discipline but added the regulatory piece of the equation, which was very different from working on LCAs. My last position as an application engineer, I had to learn all about firmware and software and how our printers used them to function. Up until this position, the only exposure I had to our printers was mainly calculating energy and paper use required for conducting an LCA and what the bill of materials consisted of. I didn't know anything about how firmware and software are used to enable printer behavior. Again, this was a steep learning curve for me. I wasn't a software or firmware engineer which is usually what an electrical or software engineer does. I didn't have to learn either of these in depth, but I had to be somewhat conversant in them to talk to our customers about them.

All the positions I discussed above show how you need to be willing to learn new things or try something completely different. I think my willingness to do this helped my career at HP and allowed me to stay with them as long as I did.

Teamwork

One of the things I liked about working at both Kellogg's and HP was the opportunity to work in teams. At Kellogg's, the team I was in included both food scientists and engineers where we worked together to develop a new product or improve an existing product to meet new market demands. It was fun and interesting to work with a diverse team of individuals from different backgrounds and experience. I knew a little about food science since I took some graduate courses in it but seeing what they did in industry was really a great experience in how the development process and problem solving were approached and carried out. When working on a project each individual brought their area of expertise and knowledge to bear on the effort. At HP most of the teams I was on were with fellow engineers, but I did get to interact with chemists, physicists, material scientists, and statisticians. Extended teams also included technicians and operators when working on manufacturing process improvements. One of the best teams I was part of was when we were doing material development with outside suppliers for inkjet printer cartridges. It was a multi-year project with a group of very talented engineers and scientists. The supplier also had a team we worked directly with that also was a group of very talented scientists. We had regular meetings, had a specific goal to achieve, and the team's communication and interactions were well organized. The team was able to deliver superior results and achieve the material development objectives we had set out to meet. It was one of those teams where everyone was energized, excited to contribute, and got along together.

Communication

This is an important area for an engineer to excel in. Most successful engineers are good communicators across and up an organization. Just being a smart person with good technical skills does not mean you will be a good communicator. It takes training and development to get good at communicating effectively. One area that most engineers will be involved in is presenting their ideas and results to management, in meetings with peers, and with customers. A successful presentation is more than just reviewing data. It needs to be engaging, to the point, and not just reading your notes. You need to know your audience and what one main point you want them to get from your presentation. We have all seen presentations with too much data and information, or the "curse of knowledge". Because you know so much about a subject, you attempt a brain dump of everything you know in the presentation. What is the point of speaking? Is it to get your point across and be heard? Show off everything you've done? Is it to prove you're the smartest person in the room? I've often seen presentations packed with information overload and techno babble. Presentations are too often packed with unnecessary information that either confuses the audience or puts them to sleep. In rare exceptions like giving a thesis presentation to academics, more information is needed. But in most professional settings, and especially when you are talking to non-engineers, eliminating excessive information avoids audience confusion and makes your message clear. Often, it's the non-technical person you need to convince once you reach a project manager level to accept what you're recommending. The non-technical person is usually who controls the project budget that you need to convince for more money or extension of the project timeline. This applies to any type of speaking, whether it be public speaking, or simply asking your boss or coworker a question. Get to the point as quickly as reasonably possible. If your boss wants a play-by-play assessment of the project details, it will be asked for specifically. Eliminating unnecessary information helps you avoid overwhelming your audience, which is likely to result in a lackluster presentation that does not produce the outcome you desire. Some of the engineers I worked with joined a local Toastmasters club to improve their public speaking skills. I would highly recommend doing something like that if you want to improve your presentation skills. I cannot emphasize enough the importance of being an effective communicator. It will be the one skill that will make you stand out the most as an engineer to management and the organization you are in.

Flexibility/Adaptability

First, we need to define the difference between flexibility and adaptability. Flexibility is more a willingness to meet others halfway let's say on a procedure. It also means you are versatile, resilient, and responsive to change. I experienced a lot of changes while working at HP. Projects and product development were always changing and I had to be flexible, willing to change with the organization and company. Adaptability is a willingness to confront or change your own ideas and preconceptions. This is one area where I saw a lot of conflict between engineers during my career. They were not willing concede when someone was challenging their ideas. Adaptability also means that you can align and fit into the corporate culture that you are in by aligning with the corporate values. Are you willing to take on a new role beyond your skills? How do you deal with unexpected work situations? Do you devise new methods to complete a task? How open and considerate are you to other views? These are all examples of being adaptable. Here are five ways to show adaptability at work: 1) establish alternative solutions when someone turns down your initial suggestion, 2) make easy transitions where you are cooperative when transitioning to new roles, 3) keep calm and confident when faced with unexpected challenges, 4) acquire new skills, 5) diversify your knowledge and avoid limiting yourself to only one area of expertise.

Problem Solving Skills

Problem solving is all about using logic, along with imagination, to make sense of a situation and come up with an intelligent solution. In fact, the best problem solvers actively anticipate potential future problems and act to prevent them or to mitigate their effects. Problem solving skills are connected to a number of other skills including: analytical skills, innovative and creative thinking, adaptability and flexibility, initiative, and resilience. I won't go into the detailed steps of problem solving since that is readily available but rather cover what makes a good problem solver in the context of an organization in a company. Good problem solvers build networks and know how to collaborate with other people and teams. They are skilled at bringing people together and sharing knowledge and information. A key attribute of a great problem solvers is that they are trusted by others.

Building a good reputation

This goes without saying for the most part, but it's amazing how I saw so many engineers not do this. They were arrogant enough to think that they knew it all and could make it happen by running over others to do it, including their managers. This might work sometimes, but in the long run, it usually doesn't turn out well. A good reputation takes a long time to build and only a short time to destroy. By showing up every day with a great attitude, willing to work hard, relate well with others, be dependable and flexible, and complete projects that you are responsible for, your reputation will grow, and you will gain favor with your colleagues and managers. This will not happen overnight, but once you have established a good reputation, guard it with your life. Reputation is a fragile thing. A lot of it, unfortunately, has to do with perception. How people perceive you is complex because most of the time it is out of your control. One thing I have found was valuable in determining how I was perceived was asking my manager, or others I worked with for feedback. They can provide you feedback and recommendations on how to improve how you are perceived. One perception other engineers had about me I found out from my manager during one of our regular one-on-one meetings we had. He said that during large review meetings I wouldn't say much so I was perceived as not being willing to contribute. It was a wrong perception, but a perception, nonetheless. So, I had to work at being more engaged during these types of meetings and speak up and contribute. These types of interactions are not always pleasant or straight forward, but necessary in building a reputation as an excellent engineer and person with character.

Fun, family, and faith, aka "work-life balance"

One thing I really appreciated about both Kellogg's and HP was the emphasis on work-life balance. They recognized that we are human beings first and employees second. And as human beings, we are more than just employees. We are spouses, parents, enjoy family activities, play sports and music, and spiritual beings with faith in God. When I went to work for Kellogg's and HP, my family went with me in that they had to move to those places with me so I could work. My work impacted the entire family, for better or for worse. My family saw me as a spouse and parent first, not an engineer. Work saw me as an engineer first and not a spouse and father, though they knew I was both. So, as an engineer at work I had to make sure that when I got home, I was a spouse and father, not an engineer. It seems straight forward to say, but it really takes effort to be engaged at home as much as I was at work.

Our social network consisted primarily around our friends and acquaintances at church. We saw it as a very important part of our lives and a high priority for us. It provided a place to grow both spiritually and socially. I think it enhanced me as an individual and as a fellow human being and also benefited my employer. It taught me the importance of character and that translated directly over to my home life and work life. Maintaining a healthy work-life balance will only enhance you as an employee. Workaholics eventually burn out or become very one dimensional. I believe that my work is a calling. I am an engineer because God gave me these abilities and a desire to do it in the first place. It keeps me humble because in believing that all my abilities come from God reminds me that I'm not the one in control, He is, and that someday I will stand accountable for how I used the gifts and talents He gave to me.

Financial Rewards

We all work to earn a living and build a good life for ourselves and our families. Engineering is a well-paying field where there is the potential to make well over six figures annually during a career. The challenge of having a good salary is to save as much of it as you can during your career. Budget like your future depends on it! I'll talk about the importance of financial planning below. You are paid well for the knowledge you bring to the company and continue to develop, contributions to the company, and your performance. Every company has a method of measuring your performance. Some are better than others, but it is measured, and you are rewarded if you perform well. Some companies also provide stock options and bonuses based on your annual performance. It can add significantly to your base salary, so it does pay to work hard, make a contribution, and have a good attitude. At HP I was fortunate to have benefited from both stock options and annual bonuses. HP also followed the industry trend of offering a 401K as a retirement plan instead of a pension and they contributed a certain percentage annually if you contributed. HP's 401K was administered by Fidelity Investments and Fidelity provided a great service for investment advice and help which I used a lot. The benefit of a 401K is that you get both a tax deferred savings plan and a way to save on annual taxes since the amount you contribute annually reduces your taxable income dollar for dollar. It worked out well for me since I had a plan and goal for saving. I used a financial planner from Edward Jones to help me formulate a retirement savings plan to meet my goal of being able to retire by age sixty-five. I would recommend shopping around for financial planner to make sure they have a good reputation and referrals. I actually retired early at age sixty-three when HP offered an enhanced early retirement package in 2019 so I was able to take the retirement package because I had stuck to my retirement savings goals. I can't emphasize enough the need to set up a retirement savings plan as soon as you can and stick with it. You never know what life may throw at you and being able to be financially secure enough to live off your investment savings brings peace of mind and security. One definition of financial wealth I heard that I like is:

"wealth is how long you can live on your savings". If you can live only a year on your savings, then you have one year's worth of wealth. If you can live on your savings for the rest of your life, then you are wealthy for the rest of your life. You notice that I don't use the word, "rich", since that is subjective. How rich you are is very dependent on what lifestyle you want to live and how much money you must spend to meet that lifestyle.

I bring up this topic because I saw many engineers who were brilliant and smart about many things, but who didn't have a clue how to manage their money or save for the future. Don't be one of them. Learn how to manage your money or find someone to help you like I did. It's the best investment of time and money you will ever make besides the investment you made in your education and career. Here is a list of books I recommend reading as they will provide a mindset about money, how to invest, and some practical guidance on savings, reducing debt, and how to be frugal, but not cheap. There are many other good books on the subject, but these are good ones to start with.

- "Richest Man In Babylon", George S Clason
- "The Millionaire Next Door", Thomas J Stanley
- "Automatic Millionaire", David Bach
- "The Little Book Of Common Sense Investing", John Bogle

EPILOGUE

———

Well, I hope you have been inspired by my unlikely story of how I became an engineer and was able to be involved in some very innovative projects and technologies in both the food and high-tech industries. I feel extremely grateful for the opportunities I had to work at these two great companies. I also have a deep respect for all the great people who work at these companies. I rubbed shoulders with operators, technicians, electricians, chemists, and physicists who were great at their jobs and without them I wouldn't have gotten as far as I did. Being an engineer is no more important than any other job. It's just a different job. I hope you've also seen the human side of an engineer too. We're not all like the characters you see on the sitcom The Big Bang Theory where they are depicted as social misfits who don't know how to interact with other people. I have seen those types during my career, and it makes me cringe, which gives us a bad name, but I have also seen many good, decent people who are relatable and great to get along with.

And if you're one of those people who think you're

not a likely candidate for being an engineer or a doctor or whatever, take heart with what you have just read about and realize that it is possible. There are many exciting career paths with many options to choose from. There are many great companies and organizations looking for conscientious, innovative people to come on board and to make a contribution. Just do it! Then someday you will have your own story to tell.

REFERENCES

1. Strecker, Tim. *Take This Job and Love It!: My Personal Journey from Full-time Ministry into Full-time Work.* Westbow Press, 2013.
2. Strecker, T.D., Cavalieri, R.P., Pomeranz, Y., Wheat Gluten and Glutenin Thermal Conductivity and Diffusivity at Extruder Temperatures, Journal of Food Science 59(6):1244 - 1246 · August 2006
3. Strecker, T.D., Cavalieri, R.P., Zollars, R., HEAT TRANSFER to and TRANSPORT PROPERTIES of WHEAT GLUTEN IN A TUBULAR REACTOR, Journal of Food Process Engineering 18(4):431 - 447 · January 2007
4. Strecker, T.D., Cavalieri, R.P., Zollars, R., Pomeranz, Y., Polymerization and Mechanical Degradation Kinetics of Gluten and Glutenin at Extruder Melt-Section Temperatures and Shear Rates, Journal of Food Science 60(3):532 - 537 · August 2006
5. https://www.battlecreekmi.gov/377/History
6. 8,469,231 Mixing rotary positive displacement pump for micro-dispensing

7. 8,070,018 Viscoelastic liquid flow splitter and methods
8. 7,377,615 Article of manufacturing including a two-part adhesive with a fluorescent dye and method of making
9. 7,178,896 Article of manufacturing including a two-part adhesive with a fluorescent dye and method of making
10. 6,935,534 Mixing rotary positive displacement pump for micro-dispensing
11. 6,691,895 Mixing rotary positive displacement pump for micro-dispensing
12. 6,386,396 Mixing rotary positive displacement pump for micro-dispensing
13. www8.hp.com › hpinfo › hpvs › OnlinePatentSales

ABOUT THE AUTHOR

Tim and his wife, Connie, live in Portland, Oregon. They have two grown children and two grandchildren. They have lived in the Pacific Northwest most of their lives and spent most of that time living in the Puget Sound area of Everett and Tacoma before moving to Oregon twenty four years ago. Tim worked as an engineer at Kellogg's in Battle Creek, MI for two years. Then he worked at the Hewlett Packard Company in Oregon and

Washington for over twenty three years where he worked in a number of engineering positions. He recently retired from HP. Connie has worked as a legal assistant and started a small cereal company selling specialty granolas. In their spare time they enjoy spending time with their family, landscaping and gardening, and music.